Blind

TO YOUR WRONG

by

a Friend of Medjugorje

SPECIAL STATEMENT

Caritas of Birmingham is not acting on behalf of the Catholic Church or placing its mission under the Church. Its mission is to reach all people of the earth. Its actions are outside of the Church done privately. It is further stated:

So as not to take for granted the credibility of the Medjugorje Apparitions, it is stated that the Medjugorje apparitions are not formally approved by the Catholic Church.

Medjugorje Status
February 2, 2021 A.D.

No attempt is intended to pre-empt the Church on the validity of the Medjugorje Apparitions. They are private revelation waiting the Church's final judgment[1]. In the interim, these private revelations **are** allowed by, and for, the faithful to have devotion to and to be spread legally by the Church. Devotion and the propagation of private revelations can be forbidden only **if** the private revelation is condemned because of anything it contains which contravenes faith and morals according to AAS 58 (1966) 1186 Congregation for the Doctrine of the Faith. Medjugorje has not been condemned nor found to have anything against faith or morals, therefore it is in the grace of the Church to be followed by the faithful. By the rite of Baptism one is commissioned and given the authority to evangelize. *"By Baptism they share in the priesthood of Christ, in His prophetic and royal mission."*[2] One does not need approval to promote or to have devotions to private revelations or to spread them when in conformity to AAS 58 (1966) 1186, as the call to evangelize is given when baptized. These apparitions have not been approved formally by the Church. Caritas of Birmingham, the Community of Caritas and all associated with it, realize and accept that the final authority regarding the Queen of Peace, Medjugorje and happenings related to the apparitions, rests with the Holy See in Rome. We at Caritas, willingly submit to that judgment. While having an amiable relationship with the Diocese of Birmingham and a friendly relationship with its bishop, Caritas of Birmingham as a lay mission is not officially connected to the Diocese of Birmingham, Alabama, just as is the Knights of Columbus.[3] The Diocese of Birmingham's official position on Caritas is neutral and holds us as Catholics in good standing.

1. The Church does not have to approve the apparitions. The Church can do as She did with the apparitions of Rue du Bac in Paris and the Miraculous Medal. The Church never approved these apparitions. She gave way to the people's widespread acceptance of the Miraculous Medal and thereby the Apparitions to St. Catherine. *Sensus Fidelium* (Latin, meaning "The Sense of the Faithful"), regarding Medjugorje, is that the "sense" of the people says that "Mary is here (Medjugorje)."
2. Catechism of the Catholic Church Second Edition.
3. The Knights of Columbus also are not officially under the Church, yet they are very Catholic. The Knights of Columbus was founded as a lay organization in 1882, with the basic Catholic beliefs. Each local council appeals to the local Ordinary to be the Chaplain. The Knights of Columbus is still a lay organization, and operates with its own autonomy.

Published with permission from SJP Lic. COB.

ISBN: 978-1-878909-38-1

Printed and bound in the United States of America.

For additional copies, contact your local bookstore or call
Caritas of Birmingham at 205-672-2000 USA.

Blind

—TO YOUR WRONG—

by

a Friend of Medjugorje

Published with permission from SJP by
CARITAS OF BIRMINGHAM
STERRETT, ALABAMA 35147 USA

About the Witness

Many who will read these books have been following the writings of a Friend of Medjugorje for years. His original and unique insights into the important events of our day have won credence in hundreds of thousands of hearts around the world, with those affecting others, thereby, touching into the millions. His moral courage in the face of so many leaders caving in to the pressures of a politically correct world is not only refreshing, but, according to tens of thousands of written testimonies over 32 years, has helped to strengthen deeply those who desire to live the fullness of their Christian faith. His insights have repeatedly proven prophetic, having their source in the apparitions of the Virgin Mary in Medjugorje. Deeply and personally influenced by the events surrounding Medjugorje, he gave himself to the prayerful application of the words of the Virgin Mary into his life. He has spoken all over the world on Our Lady's messages and how to put them into everyday life. He came to understand that Our Lady was sent by God to speak to mankind in this time because the dangers man is facing are on a scale unlike any the world has ever known since Noah and the flood. He is not an author. He is a witness of what Our Lady has shown him to testify to—first, by his life—secondly, through the written word. He is not one looking in from the outside regarding Medjugorje, but one who is close to the events—many times, right in the middle of the events about which he has written.

Originally writing to only a few individuals in 1987, readership has grown well into the millions in the United States and in over 130 foreign countries, who follow the spiritual insights and direction given through these writings.

When asked why he signs only as "a Friend of Medjugorje," he stated:

"I have never had an ambition or desire to write. I do so only because God has shown me, through prayer, that He desires this of me. So from the beginning, when I was writing to only a few people, I prayed to God and promised I would not sign anything; that the writings would have to carry themselves and not

be built on a personality. I prayed that if it was God's desire for these writings to be inspired and known, then He could do it by His Will and grace and that my will be abandoned to it.

"The Father has made these writings known and continues to spread them to the ends of the earth. These were Our Lord's last words before ascending: **'Be a witness to the ends of the earth.'** *These writings give testimony to that desire of Our Lord, to be a witness with one's life. It is not important to be known. It is important to do God's Will."*

For those who require "ownership" of these writings by the 'witness' in seeing his name printed on this work in order to give it more credibility, we, Caritas of Birmingham and the Community of Caritas, state that we cannot reconcile the fact that these writings are producing hundreds of thousands of conversions, and will easily be into the millions, through God's grace. His writings are requested worldwide from every corner of the earth. His witness and testimony, therefore, will not take credit for a work that, by proof of the impact these writings have to lead hearts to conversion, has been Spirit–inspired, with numbers increasing yearly, sweeping as a wave across the ocean. Indeed, in this case, crossing every ocean of the earth. Our Lady gave this Witness a direct message, through the Medjugorje visionary, Marija, and part of what Our Lady said to him was to **"…witness not with words but through humility…"** (Oct. 6, 1986) It is for this reason that he wishes to remain simply, "A Friend of Medjugorje."

In order to silence the voice of this witness, darkness has continually spewed out slanders to prevent souls from reading his convicting and life-changing writings. For if these writings were not so, darkness would ignore them or even lead people to them. But Jesus promised persecution to all those who follow Him, and the same will be to those who follow His Mother. *"If they persecuted me, they will also persecute you."* John 15:20

As a witness in real-time of Our Lady's time on earth, his witness and writings will continue to speak—voicing Our Lady's Way to hundreds of millions not yet born—in the centuries to come.

— Caritas of Birmingham

Acknowledgement

God alone deserves the credit for the publication of this book. It is from Him that the messages are allowed to be given through Our Lady to all of mankind. He alone deserves the praise and honor.

Table of Contents

IX   FOREWORD

XVII   PREFACE

XIX   IMPORTANT LETTER
        BEFORE YOU BEGIN

CHAPTER ONE
1   RUN TO THE ROAR

CHAPTER TWO
9   ARE YOU A THOMAS?

CHAPTER THREE
17   MEDICINE FROM HEAVEN

CHAPTER FOUR
23   A NEW LANGUAGE
      AND
      DE MONTFORT'S PROPHECY

CHAPTER FIVE
35   DECLARATION OF WAR

CHAPTER SIX
43   FAILURE OF THE USCCB

CHAPTER SEVEN
49   "NUANCED" TEACHING

CHAPTER EIGHT
57 THE FAILING OF OUR SHEPHERDS

CHAPTER NINE
63 MAN UP

CHAPTER TEN
71 CHANGE YOUR COURSE

CHAPTER ELEVEN
79 FREEDOM TO PROPAGATE

83 A DECLARATION FOR PUBLIC RECORD

91 TESTIMONIES

139 ENDNOTES

FOREWORD

This foreword contains two parts. The first part is the "Story in Brief" and the second part is "An Important Read."

THE VILLAGE SEES THE LIGHT is the title of a story which "Reader's Digest" published in February 1986. It was the first major news on a mass public scale that told of the Virgin Mary visiting the tiny village of Medjugorje, Bosnia-Hercegovina. At that time this village was populated by 400 families.

It was June 24, 1981, the Feast of John the Baptist, the proclaimer of the coming Messiah. In the evening, around 5:00 p.m., the Virgin Mary appeared to two young people, Mirjana Dragičević** and Ivanka Ivanković*. Around 6:40 p.m. the same day, Mirjana and Ivanka, along with four more young people, Milka Pavlović*, the little sister of Marija, Ivan Ivanković,

---

* Names at the time of the apparitions, they are now married with last names changed.

Vicka Ivanković*, and Ivan Dragičević saw the Virgin Mary. The next day, June 25, 1981, along with Mirjana, Ivanka, Vicka and Ivan Dragičević, Marija Pavlović* and Jakov Čolo also saw the Virgin Mary, bringing the total to six visionaries. Milka Pavlović* and Ivan Ivanković only saw Our Lady once, on that first day. These six have become known as and remain "the visionaries."

These visionaries are not related to one another. Three of the six visionaries no longer see Our Lady on a daily basis. As of October 2020, the Virgin is still appearing every day to the remaining three visionaries; that's well over 16,888 apparitions. The supernatural event has survived all efforts of the Communists to put a stop to it, and the visionaries have been the subject of many scientific studies over the span of many years, yet, the apparitions have survived, giving strong evidence that this is from God because nothing and no one has been able to stop it. For over 39 years, the apparitions have proved themselves over and over and now credibility is so favorable around the world that the burden of proof that this is authentic has shifted from those who believe to the burden of proof that it is not happening by those opposed to it. Those against the apparitions are being crushed by the fruits of Medjugorje — millions and millions of conversions which are so powerful that they are changing and will continue to change the whole face of the earth.

AN IMPORTANT READ

Many who will read this book have been following the writings of A Friend of Medjugorje for years. His original and unique insights into the important events of our day have won credence in millions of hearts around the world. His moral courage in the face of so many leaders caving into the pressures of a politically correct world is not only refreshing, but according to tens of thousands of written and verbal testimonies, has helped to deeply strengthen those who desire to live the fullness of Christianity. His insights, that are often prophetic, have their source in the apparitions of the Virgin Mary in Medjugorje. Deeply and personally influenced by a Biblical worldview and the events surrounding Medjugorje, he gave himself to the prayerful study and application into his life of the words that the Virgin Mary has been speaking over the past quarter of a century. He discovered that She has come to speak to mankind in this time because the dangers we face are on a scale unlike any the world has ever known. Millions have been deeply affected by his writings.

While reading this book, one is free to ignore the happenings of the phenomenon of Medjugorje, but in doing so, one would be choosing to ignore over 30 years of scientific testing, from 1981 until the present. The most recent comprehensive study was conducted by a team of French scientists in 2005, with the most modern means of testing available from the scientific world. Those findings affirm that while science cannot say it is the Virgin Mary appearing, science **"can support the absence of deception."** The scientific teams have determined that these occurrences are of supernatural origin. Over 30 years of testing, evaluation, and the proof of changed lives are a testament to the reality that God is speaking to the world today through Medjugorje.

For those who approach this writing with skepticism concerning the apparitions of the Virgin Mary, whether you are of a faith that is inclined to reject such apparitions or a nonbeliever, we suggest that you not let that deter you from reading this book, but simply read the messages of the Virgin Mary as comments such as a pastor would make. We say this because there are a great many things that are threatening our nation's future and that knowledge is important for all men to understand, especially Americans because of the position God has placed us in the world. The truths contained within this writing have an important contribution to make in the ongoing national dialogue that will determine whether America will continue on the path of destruction it has been on for the past several decades or will find the will to return to the ideals and the vision of their founding fathers. <u>The David Answer</u>_{TM} places in the hands of the reader the answer by which all our woes can be corrected, when each Christian accepts to change his life and live according to all the precepts given to us by God. In doing so we will be contributing more to the future peace and security of the United States of America than any government, military, agency or program. For as the author often writes, "a people are not so much protected by their armaments as they are by their way of life."

In the United States of America, the way of life of *"we the people"* has always been based in the living of Christian principles, even for non-Christians. If we wish to have the protection of God that we have always enjoyed in this nation, if we wish America to be saved from all of the impending evils that are surrounding us, then America must return to living Christianity in its fullness. By doing so, we will become God's children of light again, and He will reach down from the Heavens and save us. We thank God for allowing Our Lady, the Queen of Peace, to be with us in these trying times, as His ambassador from Heaven. May we heed Her words to return to the Father, who is waiting for us that He may once again bestow His blessings upon us.

—The Publisher

PREFACE

In the following writing, a Friend of Medjugorje takes the United States' bishops to task as never before. Witnessing the "Time of Grace" of Our Lady's apparitions winding down, after almost 40 years, and seeing the desert of what our world has become, a Friend of Medjugorje considers it an immeasurable tragedy that the bishops have yet to give a green light to Our Lady. Heaven came with a solution for all the world's needs, and it was ignored by the shepherds.

Addressing the bishops' silence, their inertia, their fear, their betrayal of Christ through their rejection of His Mother's visitations—a Friend of Medjugorje is blunt in his castigation of their inaction. Having put his own reputation, and the mission God entrusted to him, on the chopping block over and over again, in obedience to what God requires of him to speak, after almost 40 years, he has little patience for the recklessness by which the bishops have dealt with Medjugorje. A Friend of Medjugorje has paid the painful costs of being a witness and a voice for Our Lady, while experiencing, at the same time, the prospering and building of his mission—without any help from the Church for these almost 40 years with the Community of Caritas, the Extended Community and a worldwide following. He, therefore, has the ability to speak and write as no other, outside of the six Medjugorje visionaries. He stands with courage and moral leadership in confronting the evils of our day.

Yet, his indictment of the bishops is not without mercy, for even today, they could decide to open the doors of their dioceses to the messages of Our Lady that are medicine for the nations. The big question is, will they? Their actions over these almost 40 years gives the answer. They have said, "no," to Our Lady.

—The Community of Caritas

IMPORTANT LETTER
BEFORE YOU BEGIN

This following letter was sent from a priest friend of a Friend of Medjugorje after he read the book you are holding, <u>Blind to Your Wrong</u>. He wanted to show his support and agreement with what a Friend of Medjugorje expressed concerning the leadership of the Church in this turbulent time in the history of the Church and of the world.

Dear Friend,   *February 15, 2021*

"In your latest writing you are a modern-day John the Baptist, speaking truth to power! The tragic tale that is recent Church history is nothing less than a spectacular, diabolically orchestrated failure in leadership. I used to think the bishops were just tone deaf…now I fear that their deafness has been, and continues to be, a willful choice. The truth is many of them are so morally bankrupt, compromised, weak or just plain wicked that they simply swim along in the polluted tide of our totally lost culture. These

times we live in are a 'satanic masterpiece.' You are part of the pushback against that tide of evil.

"The good news is the Church belongs to Jesus and He has given us a Mother! Grass roots spiritual movements and communities are springing up. These Marian saints will be instrumental in the Triumph of the Immaculate Heart in these last days. Just as the great St. Louis de Montfort prophesied 350 years ago and Our Lady has spoken: 'Through you I will Triumph!' Pray! Pray! Pray!

"Thank you for keeping the authentic, saving messages and spirit of the Queen of Peace alive in our world. Your work and Community shine Her light in the darkness! God bless you in Christ!"

> *With Much Love and Respect,*
> *Father (Anonymous)*

It is signed "Anonymous" to protect the identity of the priest so that no reprisal could come against him for his statements.

"WILL THE BISHOPS EVEN HAVE THE BACKBONE TO READ THIS THROUGH??? *Perhaps it could be read to them in the Confessional... Thank you a Friend of Medjugorje for writing the words on many, many peoples' minds. May they ring from our lips to the shepherd's ears! May God have mercy on us all. Thank you Caritas! All my love to Our Lady to you!"*

Lorraine
Micco, FL

CHAPTER ONE

Run to the Roar

David Barton, an evangelical author and speaker, said the following on a recent broadcast entitled, *"Run to the Roar."* He begins by saying that male lions are not as fast as female lions, yet the two together have a strategy to capture their prey. The King of the Beasts will go on one side of a large grassy plain and roar. The roar is so loud that it can be heard five to eight miles away. The female lions, who are faster and better killers, await on the other side of the plain. The roar of the male lion scares the prey right into the claws of the female lions. If the animals were wise, they would run to the roar instead of away from the roar. The spiritual point being made is that our Christian leaders do the same; in fear, they run away from the roar of the enemies, instead of confronting the enemies and with God's help, defeat them. Barton explains why in the following:

"As we know in the Scriptures, there are two very different places that we will spend Eternity. There is Heaven and there is hell. They are both very real…Who goes to hell? Revelation 21:8 says in the first part that:

'_____, _____, the faithless, the detestable, the murderers, the immoral, the sorcerers, the idolators, and all liars go to that lake of fire.'

"Now look at all the bad stuff up there, murderers and liars and sorcerers; that's some really bad stuff, except you'll notice that [the first words in the verse were skipped.]. What is the first group that God sends to hell? The first group says:

'the <u>cowards</u> and the <u>fearful</u>.'

"Now, everybody else up there is there for what they did, liars or murderers or perjurers or whatever [they may be.]. The first two are there for what they didn't do, for lacking backbone because they didn't have backbone, because they weren't courageous, because they were fearful. That's interesting to me, that the first group that God says, 'I don't want you guys around me at all,' are the people who have no backbone, the people who won't stand up…the cowards and the fearful. That is, again, running to the roar. Cowards and fearful will not run to the roar. They don't want to engage; they don't want to be in that battle. They don't like battles. That's not who we are. If we're going to do what God wants done for Christians, and for the Church, and for the State, and for the Nation, we're going to have to learn to run to the roar. We are going to have to start engaging in a way that

we have not engaged with before. We've been
playing defense for about 40 years and we
have seen our country slowly taken from us."[1]

Bishops—everything tragically happening right now, in real time, with the **Church**, our **nation** and in the **world**, you are responsible for. I lay it before your feet on behalf of the peasants in the pew and the other lost sheep who are not in the pews, but who are also under your care. We see little honesty in the grade you would give yourselves as shepherds. This writing is not a judgement about you, because that is God's dominion alone. But we peasants in the pew are giving you a report card. We give you an F minus. You have failed miserably in recognizing what is right in front of you and you did nothing.

St. Paul said:

> ***"You stupid Galatians! Who has put***
> ***you under a spell?...Are you so stu-***

pid? After beginning with the spirit, are you now ending with the flesh?"

Galatians 3:3

Bishops, your answers are not in the stupid **U**nited **S**tates **C**onference of **C**atholic **B**ishops (USCCB), filled with committees and so-called experts who get you to sign on and adopt their non-convicting programs and solutions to problems, all the while producing no results in the way of conversions of souls. You are taking care of the flesh, while souls are declining, emaciated, and lacking nourishment for conversion. You, the bishops, are **to be** the experts. It is the Holy Spirit who has descended upon and anointed you. Are you stifling the Holy Spirit in you? You let the attorneys run the diocese instead of giving the flock a moral road to follow.

For example, you don't need stupid "talking head" committees to tell you, as bishops, what to do with former Vice President, Joe Biden and Communion. Biden, as a Catholic, publicly declares himself a defender of the "right to abortion" and creates public policies to maintain this "right," which is condemned by the Catholic Church. Recently, on November 17, 2020, the head of the USCCB, Archbishop Jose Horacio Gomez, cowardly and fearfully, side-stepped this issue and other concerns of Biden's policies by appointing "a committee" to make a study and recommendations for bishops to follow regarding whether or not Biden should be denied Holy Communion.

What is so difficult in dealing with Biden? Archbishop Gomez runs for the cover of a committee. Shame on him and all the bishops who stayed silent, letting the committee and their advisors form the judgement instead of just following the laws of the Church, decisively and immediately.[2] On December 4, 2020, Archbishop Charles Chaput, in the periodical, *First Things*, warned that individual bishops, who publicly announce their intention to give Joe Biden Holy Communion, risk "a serious disservice" to Biden and to the rest of America's bishops.[3] The USCCB seeks, through study solution committees of so-called experts, empty solutions which are devoid of grace. You are purposely blind to the fact that the answers these committees "commit" to have not worked for decades.

"My heart has been so very heavy for so long as I have watched the downfall of the Church and I feel like a prisoner for my strong warrior feelings for Our Lady. I thank you so much for standing up to the bishops for their retreatment to safeness! I keep thinking about how did the people who were in the crowds shouting Crucify Him on Friday and waving their palm branches the Sunday before, feel as the veils of hatred were lifted and they finally realized what they had done. We are right back there! May God protect us to do what is needed to save souls."

Gail
Fallatin, TN

CHAPTER TWO

Are You a Thomas?

If bishops knew truth, they could give a clear, precise answer/solution instantly, as Jesus did. In 2004, I spoke with then Bishop Raymond Burke of the La Crosse, Wisconsin Diocese, before he was named Archbishop of St. Louis. Burke grew up on a farm in rural Wisconsin. He believed there was value in returning to a more agrarian way of life for the Church, which was our intent and purpose for meeting with him. Later, we met in Rome when Archbishop Burke was appointed Prefect of the Apostolic Signatura in 2008, the highest court in the Catholic Church. Burke was made a Cardinal two years later by Pope Benedict XVI. At that time, I discussed with Burke the difficulty our mission was experiencing through the restrictions by the bishops. Cardinal Burke did not go and reflect on committee rulings to me. Rather, he gave strong, clear direction without compromise. There was no "maybe" or "so-so." He said what he said with the power of his discernment, not relying on anyone else's opinion, but in truth.

Cardinal Burke is brave and retains a courage that the Church very much needs, rather than what we have now in the bishops who straddle the fence, refusing to make definitive stands on so many critical issues of our day. Committing the "sin of nuance." The courageous "Burkes'" are one in a hundred. The strength of the Body of the Church has been weakened by poor discernment, a fear to stand up against the world, and for some, an acceptance of scandalous sin within the Church. This has happened under your reign as bishops. You avoid making a decision and pass if off to committees. Your answers ought not to be in or through the USCCB.

If answers were to be found in the USCCB, why are we in <u>this</u>, our time, clearly experiencing Divine Intervention? Divine Intervention? Where? How? Why? What you should be the first to see, you are blind to it because you seek only those answers that the world will approve. The key word again, "nuance," to pass the buck instead of confrontation. The world assembles and implements worldly solutions, rejecting the spiritual. You are bankrupting the Church. Don't roll your eyes about what you are about to read because somewhere in the near future you may want to sear your eyes out for what you did not want to see. Your answers haven't worked.

Where are the answers? They are in a mandate. Forty years of Divine Intervention from the spiritual realm, about to manifest into the physical realm.

Your answers are in Medjugorje.

Your answers are in the messages given in Medjugorje.

Your answers are in the Queen of Peace.

Your answers are in the infallible "fact" that Our Lady is appearing every day for almost 40 years.

Infallible?

Your lack of understanding, in this moment of Divine Intervention, is such a lack of faith that perhaps you need to adopt the name "Bishop Thomas," after the apostle Thomas who out of all the apostles, was the one who did not believe in the Resurrection.

> *"But [Thomas] said to them, 'Unless I see the mark of the nails in his hands and put my finger into the nail marks and put my hand into his side, I will not believe.'"* John 20:25

Will you not believe unless the Virgin Mary appears to you personally? ***"Blessed are those who believe without seeing,"*** the Gospel says. Your answers are in the conclusions made by a multitude of scientists who studied and tested the visionaries, putting them through the grinder, leaving no stone unturned in their search for the truth.* These scientists reached the verdict that the six visionaries are seeing something not of this world. After 23 years of utilizing the most advanced scientific methods and tests, the scientists made their final conclusion in 2005, having exhausted every scientific test possible. The team of scientists' final, infallible conclusion was simply stated. The visionaries:

"are absent of deceit."

Of the 22 main scientists, plus others, several issued **a warning** to the Church, saying the claims of the visionaries should be taken seriously. Some of

* Go to medjugorje.com - Scientific Studies: https://www.medjugorje.com/medjugorje/scientific-studies.html

the scientists were atheists and became believers through their tests and studies. At this point, it is pertinent for the "Bishop Thomas'" to review the definition of "infallible."

Infallible: incapable of making mistakes or being wrong.

"Thank you for your leadership in addressing our shepherds. I wholeheartedly agree. Most of them have missed the time of their visitation. As a governing body, they have utterly failed us and firmly placed us in the cattle cars of the anti-human, antichrist globalist agenda, with which Biden is absolutely tied. The Red Dragon of Communism has spread its errors over the whole world and is preparing to enslave us physically in addition to the spiritual enslavement of confused Catechesis (ie: 'socialist justice') we have been enduring so long under the USCCB. Keep fighting. I unite my prayers and longings to yours."

L.T.
Dunlap, TN

CHAPTER THREE

Medicine From Heaven

Medjugorje is bigger than "real;" it is Biblical. Medjugorje is the open door into Revelation. Yet, while you reject or ignore and are indifferent to Medjugorje, it is the science that validates its truth to such mentalities. Yet, you hypocritically accept the very questionable "science" of wearing the mask, the science that is not infallible, nor provable, as many experts are showing. You, our shepherds, are supposed to be protecting your flock, but you blindly accept the masks and the controls being forced upon the Church, without questioning who or what is behind it all. You turn away from the above, 100% scientific conclusion the visionaries are seeing a Supernatural Being in front of them, while putting your faith in the mask, when there are many scientific objections coming out regarding wearing the mask. More and more scientists and doctors are showing scientific data that masks are dangerous and harmful to one's health on several levels.

For example, the continuous wearing of masks, breathing in one's own carbon dioxide, is damaging the end of brain nerves through lack of sufficient oxygen. There is great concern that wearing masks for hours a day will, 10 years from now, lead to an epidemic of dementia. Again, while you bishops abide by the mandate of the mask, you remain indifferent to Our Lady's plans for the healing of the world with the answers right in front of you. You are more concerned with saving the flesh, and all the while disregarding what the soul needs. The medicine Heaven has sent for the Church and world, through the presence and messages of Our Lady, cures every ill. Jesus said:

"Do not be afraid of those who kill the body but cannot kill the soul; rather be afraid of God, who can destroy both body and soul in hell."

Matthew 10:28

Medjugorje is straight from Heaven and is the vaccine against evil, yet you won't prescribe it. But you will recommend the agenda of the coronavirus vaccine, which will result in the advancement of darkness, as many **will see** in the future. It is a tool to damage one's spiritual health, even to the point of risking their Eternal Life for death of the soul. Medjugorje is your answer, with its hundreds of millions of conversions. These conversions are not shallow, but deep conversions. Said even better, they are radical life-changing conversions. They are conversions such as the likes of Mary Magdalene, the corrupter of men, and the apostle Matthew, the despicable tax collector. All peoples from all walks of life, those from all faiths, from the greatest sinners, the spiritually lethargic, the dregs of society to the top of the tier of society elites—all walks of mankind are represented in the people who have been converted through Medjugorje.

But through the decades, you dare not touch Medjugorje. Actually, it may be better you hadn't. You would have redefined what Our Lady desired because you are too indoctrinated with "worldly" theology and skewed interpretations of Church doctrines to understand the new language, delivered from Heaven, language that the learned think is too simple and repetitious. No, this language, this new communication, is something that has never happened since the beginning of time. The world is seeing a "first-born" miracle, something that has never happened in all of history; a new language that speaks to us in words we recognize, but with a Divine ability for everyone to be able to hear Our Lady communicate to us individually. A new efficacy birthed by the Queen of Peace to communicate to all Her children that are devoted to Her. One message can speak to a whole group or to each of us individually. The same message will also speak to you the next day, month, year, etc., with a different meaning.

"Finally...thank you. Outstanding message."

Beth

Fishersville, VA

CHAPTER FOUR

A New Language
and
De Montfort's Prophecy

God has given to Our Lady a new, profound efficacy that the world has never seen, for the Mother of all to help us to hear Her and to break through the distracting noise of today's technological prodigies and electronics that dangerously distance the world and souls further and further away from God. God had to give us a new communication to cancel the satanic chatter that satan has over all of Our Lady's children. Our Lady said:

April 4, 1985

> **"...I wish to keep on giving you messages as it has never been in history from the beginning of the world..."**

Our Lady said three very important things regarding Her above message.

1. **"...I wish to keep on giving you messages as it has never been..."**

2. **"in history..."**

3. **"from the beginning of the world..."**

You have missed almost 40 years, in real time, when Heaven has "snowed down" grace, through Our Lady's presence and words as never before. As a snowflake, to the naked eye, is a plain, simple white dot, but under a microscope, its splendor and purity is revealed, so too Our Lady's messages, to the naked eye, are plain and simple words, but through the microscope of prayer, their splendor and purity are revealed. Looking at Our Lady's messages, through the soul's microscope, reveals their profound beauty that literally speaks to a heart through grace. This mystery, of which I have written for decades, exposed in the words written here, is why Our Lady said these are **"messages as never in history"** in order to save the world.

As said above, these almost 40 years passing is a tragedy for you bishops, but there is a greater tragedy in that you have not let the peasants in the pew freely propagate what is on Heaven's front burner to convert the world. It's not even on your agenda with your conferences and committees, which are busy being busy, producing nothing but a weakening Church. Some of these peasants in the pew are a chosen body, raised up as apostles, not in a symbolic way, but literally, to be apostles of Our Lady, just as St. Louis de Montfort prophesied when he said—Our Lady would come to raise up apostles of the latter days.

> *"Towards the end of the world ... Almighty God and His holy Mother are to raise up saints who will surpass in holiness most other saints as much as the cedars of Lebanon tower above little shrubs."* [4]

But what does that apply to? De Montfort continues:

> *"These great souls filled with grace and zeal*
> *will be chosen to oppose the enemies of God*
> *who are raging on all sides. They will be ex-*
> *ceptionally devoted to the Blessed Virgin.*
> *Illumined by Her light, strengthened by Her*
> *spirit, supported by Her arms, sheltered under*
> *Her protection, they will fight with one hand*
> *and build with the other."* [5]

Bishops, does this not apply now?   What does de Montfort say?

"They will be <u>true apostles</u> of the lat-ter times..."

Bishops, Thomas', why did de Montfort state, approximately 300 years ago, what Our Lady of Medjugorje has repeatedly said in our time, referring to **"my apostles?"** Our Lady has called Her "true apostles" of this time, mentioning **"my"** **"apostles"** at least 153 times in Her messages. De

Montfort, described 300 years ago, what is exactly happening now, in our time, through Medjugorje. De Montfort says Mary's first coming, being born years before Jesus, naturally preceded Jesus' First Coming, and that Our Lady was scarcely known through Her life on earth. But there would be a second coming of Our Lady, preceding Jesus' Second Coming.[6]

De Montfort makes clear that Our Lady must be known before She comes on the scene in Her second coming. And She has become known more and more throughout the centuries. How? Through Guadalupe, in Mexico, at Rue de Bac in Paris, France (where She made Her request of the Miraculous Medal to be worn around the neck so people will see it, making Her more known) Lourdes, France, and Fatima, Portugal, as well as other, minor apparitions throughout history. All of these apparitions were for the purpose of making Our Lady known and loved for the time of Mary that God ordained to prepare the world for Her Son's Second Coming. De Montfort wrote:

> **"Mary scarcely (hardly known) <u>appeared in the first coming of Christ</u>... But in the second coming of Jesus Christ, <u>Mary must be known and openly revealed by the Holy Spirit so that Jesus may be known, loved and served through Her</u>."**[7]

All previous apparitions of Our Lady are paralleling the method of the First Coming of the Messiah. A long string of prophets, from Adam all the way to the last and greatest prophet, John the Baptist, prepared the way for the Coming of the Messiah. In the same way, all the above-mentioned apparitions of Our Lady, ending with Fatima, the last and greatest prophetic apparition, were for the purpose of preparing for the time, not of the coming of the Messiah, but the coming of the Woman of Revelation.

Do you need a sign? Fatima is the "John the Baptist," the last prophetic apparition before Our Lady's coming to Medjugorje, Her last apparitions on earth. And to confirm this even further, Our Lady's apparitions in Medjugorje began on June 24, 1981, on the Feast of John the Baptist! Do you get the message, the sign? But Our Lady told the visionaries 'not to celebrate' the anniversary of the Medjugorje apparitions on June 24th, John the Baptist's feast day, but rather to celebrate the anniversary of Her coming on the day of Her second apparition, June 25th. This gives a clear connection. John the Baptist, the last prophet heralding the coming of the Messiah, connected with the meaning and purpose of Fatima to prepare the world for the coming of the final fulfillment of all the apparitions of the Woman of Revelation.

Bishops think: Why did Our Lady say the following in Medjugorje?

May 2, 1982

"I have come to call the world to conversion for the last time…"

May 2, 1982

"…I will not appear any more on this earth."

This is what Medjugorje is, bishops. You have missed the train. It is time for you to listen to Our Lady's apostles, who sit scattered throughout your churches, the peasants in the pews. It bears repeating what St. Louis de Montfort wrote: Our Lady preceded Jesus the first time and Our Lady is preceding Jesus the second time for Her Son's Second Coming. De Montfort:

"Mary must be known and openly revealed by the Holy Spirit so that Jesus may be known, loved and served through Her."[8]

But the Church teaches not to dwell on the Second Coming of Jesus, etc.

I was working with the top producer for ABC 20/20, hosted by Barbara Walters and Hugh Downs, on a Caritas production film in Medjugorje, *The Lasting Sign*, with Martin Sheen, in 1988. He asked me: *"Do you think these apparitions are to prepare for the Second Coming?"* I answered, *"There is no question that they are."* He then asked, *"When?"* I answered, *"That is the big question: 5 years, 50 years, 500 years? We don't know. But I tell you, these apparitions are in preparation for the Second Coming of Jesus."* I, a peasant in the pew, stated that 33 years ago* when there were no signs like there are today, especially in being able to see now the advancement of an antichrist system. Nobody saw it back then. I saw it clearly because Our Lady made it known to me through Her messages. Why are you blind to it now when it is in your face? Even

---

* From 2021.

the Medjugorje world did not buy into the idea that Our Lady's presence in Medjugorje is for the purpose of crushing the serpent's head, in preparation for Her Son's Second Coming. Forty years gone! Now you can stick your finger in Our Lady's Seven Sorrows and stick your hand in Her heart where the sword pierced.

"We have followed Our Lady's Messages from the beginning and have presented ourselves in Medjugorje.

"With a strong and fervent belief in Her Messages, our lives have been changed. We, too, are disgusted and dismayed at the lack of leadership from our bishops and cardinals. Our fervent, daily prayer is for the conversion of hearts, salvation of souls, and an end to the lukewarmness which exists in our Church and its members. May God have Mercy on us and our country!"

FKD
Wheaton, IL

CHAPTER FIVE

Declaration of War

How do we know we are at the fulfillment of Our Lady's work through Her apparitions? First, Our Lady said these are the last apparitions, and Our Lady said:

January 25, 1997

"...this time is my time..."

Was St. Louis de Montfort in disillusionment? Was he making this up? You have words from an official canonized saint describing everything of what Our Lady is about in Medjugorje, down to the detail of matching the present conditions of the Church and in the world and you do nothing, trusting the works of the USCCB, instead of Our Lady and giving a green light to Her apostles. If you don't believe the prophecies of St. Louis de Montfort, then you won't believe in Our Lady of Medjugorje. If you believe de Montfort, you have to believe in Our Lady of Medjugorje.

You of the USCCB have dumped our beautiful nation in the trash heap. We are not going to sit anymore in the pew, lethargically, while the world burns down, nation by nation. We are declaring war against your mentalities, not your faculties, because we need the Sacraments, and because we know that even an evil priest still brings Jesus down to the altar. I am not vilifying you; you vilify yourselves. I am expressing the deep concern that I, along with millions, feel of your failures in protecting your flocks.

In Israel, I watched a shepherd tending his flock. The shepherd followed the sheep. The sheep knew how to seek out the best grass to eat. The shepherd is there to protect them from predators, but the sheep know what to eat. Forty years of rich food for our souls and our shepherds do not open the gate to the pasture to allow us to graze on the food of the Virgin Mary, Her messages of Medjugorje. You have displayed how you lost the power of discernment, not recognizing God's plans to save the world through the Queen of Peace of Medjugorje. The peasants in the pews have discerned and recognized God's plan for the world even while being thwarted by our bishops, thwarted through your indifference, silence, unjust condemnations, nonbelief, and lacking the sentiments to understand the needs of your flock.

You, bishops, keep bringing up the abominable former Cardinal Theodore McCarrick and say you are being transparent. Move on from the trash heap and go to the answers found in Our Lady. We peasants in the pew are fed up and at the end of our rope. You have proven you are not going to change your mentalities, therefore, the only thing that is going to save you is martyrdom. You, as bishops, are setting yourselves up **for a great reset.** You are about to get dethroned. You have created what our nation and other nations are now suffering from, a takeover of the good, by a rebellion of the Left, nurtured by you.

Catholic Joe Biden —	Vice President* of the United States
Catholic John Roberts —	Chief Justice of the Supreme Court
Catholic Sonia Sotomayor —	Supreme Court Justice
Catholic Nancy Pelosi —	Speaker of the House

and how many others?

All the above "Catholics" abused their positions, putting into law morally abhorrent, murderous and offensive policies that are leading this nation towards Divine Judgment.

While a few of you, bishops, a micro number, made statements against their sinful action, not one

---

* Biden is not the President and only sitting in the position by provable fraud, which is another of your sins of silence. Examine the evidence, bishops.

bishop has publicly and officially excommunicated any one of the above mentioned. Your silence is an endorsement. Your silence is not only an embarrassment, it is shameful. Your silence is an odor of stench that makes a pig pen smell fragrant. You must now own what is happening in our nation. You propagated and grew the power of the enemies of God and the Church that these enemies use now to kill babies. What is the big deal about marching and carrying a sign? *Jesus made a whip and drove the sacrilege out of the Temple.* The "Left" is fine with your March for Life marches. Much more should be happening.

You, bishops, try to stop the murdering through the corrupt legal system, instead of stopping it by stating, with all the authority given to you by God as one of His apostles, stating that, *"abortion will not continue over my dead body."* Do you know how many would follow you? But you will never know this because you won't do it, not for the sin of abortion, or euthanasia, or legalized, perverted, abominable false unions masked as marriage. You have a clear option. You were given the power of excommunication, but you won't use it. You have propagated and grown a leftist rebellion against this once good and holy nation. You have deformed the mentality of millions of people through a perverted "social justice" teaching that is not of Jesus. Your "social justice" mentality contradicts the teach- ings of Christ because it is a *"Socialist"* justice. This has damaged the worldwide Church. It is a disease spawned by you. You have created a massive num- ber of people whose mentality is that they believe they are victims. You allowed the Church to decline through your Leftist, secular, Communist, "Socialist justice" teachings pervading the Church, instead of teaching "Biblical justice." This, coupled with your silence, has led to the tragedy we are seeing engulf- ing our nation today. Silence is one of your great- est sins, hiding behind the USCCB that metes out decrees, resulting in nothing but a declining Church that takes advice from evil actors and adapts to their anti-Christ recommendations. The greatness of you being learned falls in the shadow of a man who most of you bishops, despise, even hate. A man whose power of discernment is so superior to you, bishops, that yours can be classified as artistic, even spastic discernment. That man said:

> *"The radical ideology attacking our country advances under the banner of social justice. But in truth, it would demolish both justice and society. It would transform justice into an instrument of division and vengeance, and it would turn our free and inclusive society into a place of repression, domination, and exclusion."*
>
> *President Donald John Trump*
> *July 3, 2020 — Mt. Rushmore*

Ask yourself why Trump hits the bulls-eye and you don't even hit the target.

"Yes, the Church hierarchy has failed us.
With the prophesies from Fatima and with
Medjugorje. I see a revival in other Christian
denominations but not here in our Catholic
Church. Our flock lacks leadership. As Moth-
er Mary continues to tell us pray,pray, pray."

T
Belmont, NH

CHAPTER SIX

Failure of the USCCB

In December 2020, I wrote in my writing, *"What Does Our Lady Have to Do With It? Everything,"* regarding you bishops going along with influencers surrounding the USCCB.

> *"Among the bishops who do voice disapproval of what the left is doing, their protests are generally scant, weak and almost apologetic. They are either afraid of being accused of being political, don't want to be tied up in controversy, or they sway the Church's teachings to fit their beliefs. For example, it's okay for the Democrat Party to slide by the murder of babies because the party is more for alleviating poverty, a skewed doctrine of Socialism*

*and of the antichrist, **"you will always have the poor."** For decades, the United States Catholic Conference of Bishops (USCCB) has drunk the Kool-Aid from John Carr, Director of the Initiative on Catholic Social Thought and Public Life, who worked for decades as the bishop's conference advisor on issues of justice and peace. Carr began by putting together what has become known as, 'Faithful Citizenship,' in 1976, published now for 50 years. Carr convinced our bishops, priests and religious to teach, preach and form the conscience of political life.*

*"Carr, a product of Georgetown University, directed an initiative on Catholic social thought and public life, much of which set the Church on a progressive (Leftist Socialist) trajectory. As a result of many advisors like Carr, the USCCB **prostitutes** itself to be a voice for an agenda that aligns itself with the Left and away*

from traditional Catholicism. Using the same tactics as those on the Left in government, the advisors come up with programs and documents with foggy, slick, glib language so that the USCCB can adopt it without alarming the faithful to how far Left the bishops are taking the Church, rejecting many of the Church's Sacred Teachings.

"On November 7, 2020, in an official statement, that the head of the USCCB, Archbishop of Los Angeles, Jose Gomez, offered Biden congratulations for winning the presidency even though President Trump had not conceded, and with evidence of massive voter fraud being reported before the election was even finished. The confirmation by the USCCB of Biden confirms the preceding words of how the 'curtains of power' around the bishops have entrapped many bishops to go along with implementing programs that are

Socialist, corrupt and destructive to the Catholic Church. Yes, that is on your own USCCB's website.[9] Therefore, it is in the USCCB's mentalities, teachings and the formation of the flock of Jesus Christ."[10]

Even though Carr's satanic directives are 50 years old and not one bishop condemned it, his heretical thoughts have infiltrated and reign over hundreds of bishops, allowing themselves to be corrupted. Carr recently said in his defense of voting for Joe Biden for president in November 2020:

"There may be times when a Catholic who rejects a candidate's unacceptable position even on policies promoting an intrinsically evil act may reasonably decide to vote for that candidate for other morally grave reasons."[11]

What is the fruit of such thinking? Souls languishing and the destruction of the world cultures. Everything is dealt with "nuances"—in other words, stay in the middle, don't take sides, etc. But bishops respond, "We are pro-life." Why are Biden, Roberts, Sotomayor, Pelosi and a hundred more Catholics in influential and powerful positions not touched by your testimony? You, bishops, state, like a sissy, we are pro-life. So what? You witness comfort Christianity. Jesus taught *convicting* Christianity. You have compromised too much for the sake of a false peace that now ends up in war. We, the flock of Jesus, are the casualties. However, we will not go to victimhood because Our Lady has told us injustices always existed.

June 27, 1981

> **"...do not be afraid of injustices. They have always existed."**

June 25, 1988

> **"...Little children, love bears everything bitter and difficult for the sake of Jesus Who is love..."**

"THANK YOU! I felt like getting up and cheering that someone finally said it as it is. I hope and pray that Our Lady cleans out the hierarchy…they are doing such a disservice to the flock. Their duplicity and 'nuanced' approach is sickening. So thank you for clearly stating the Truth. May Our Lady and Our Lord bless you and keep you and give you peace…and give us wisdom and peace as we fight the good fight—without our bishops. THEY are the problem!!!"

KM

CHAPTER SEVEN

"Nuanced" Teaching

Your Socialist justice is criminal. satan makes great use of this tool you give to him. The Left vilifies Christians and Conservative, praying people. We are the ones they label the haters, the intolerants, the racists and white supremacists. Incredibly, even those who are black, if they are Conservative Christians and supporters of true values, are also labeled racist, intolerant and traitors by the Left, even labeling them as white supremacists, and "turncoats." To be a Christian is to discriminate. What? Why? Because Jesus discriminated. Jesus, if He walked the earth today, would be labeled a racist and a white supremist (some actually call Him that today), because He called a Canaanite woman not a "dog" but inferred the whole race of Canaanites were dogs.

"Leaving that place, Jesus withdrew to the region of Tyre and Sidon. A Canaanite woman from that vicinity came to him, crying out, 'Lord, Son of David, have mercy on me! My daughter is demon-possessed and suffering terribly.' Jesus did not answer a word. So his disciples came to him and urged him, 'Send her away, for she keeps crying out after us.' He answered, 'I was sent only to the lost sheep of Israel.' The woman came and knelt before him. 'Lord, help me!' she said. He replied, 'It is not right to take the children's bread and toss it to the dogs.' 'Yes, it is, Lord,' she said. 'Even the dogs eat the crumbs that fall from their master's table.' Then Jesus

said to her, 'Woman, you have great faith! Your request is granted.' And her daughter was healed at that moment." Matthew 15:21–28

Christians are to be discriminating, which means: to recognize a distinction, to differentiate. As a Christian you must discriminate in what the culture accepts or rejects, and while the Christian is always ready to accept and love the person, at the same time, he discriminates against one's open, flagrant sin. Christians, themselves, have to be discriminate of themselves when they are living contrary to God's Laws and therefore, seek forgiveness for their sins. The good Christian is intolerant of his own sins, yet he is to love himself as a creature created by God.

Likewise, we know to hate and be intolerant of the sin but to love the sinner. We are called to convict hearts through our witness. Identifying sin and teaching that certain behaviors degrade mankind, is not discrimination against the person, but against the sin. Again, discrimination is defined as—"the act of distinguishing: the act of observing a difference." Many bishops who say they would accept the sinner but not the sin are lying. How many of you bishops have publicly denounced Biden's policies and made it clear that Biden's policies will further protect abortion rights? I can assure you that there are thousands of Catholics who are unaware of this due to your silence.

Every man sins and the Sacrament of Confession is the remedy. But when a man flagrantly promotes sin and refuses to repent, you hide behind the USCCB, favoring "nuanced" teachings, so that you do not have to confront the backlash of the rebellious Leftists, those both in our culture and those in our own Church. Will this inaction lead you to the grave, worst still, to the gallows? You should have distinguished what Biden is for and, therefore, discriminate and guide the people to vote against

Biden. How many bishops condemned Biden's sin for "marrying" two men in his own home when he was Vice President and blatantly publicized it to the world? How many bishops have announced not to give him Communion?

Yes, there are a few bishops who did condemn Biden's actions, and we know who they are because they have made public statements. But it is not enough. It needs to go further; it needs to go to excommunication. You cannot just say, *"I don't accept the sin. I'm not one of those bishops,"* as if that is enough. Excommunication is to put the sinner on notice that he is consigned to hell if he refuses to change what he's been excommunicated for. It is to shake his soul. Excommunication is a last resort act of mercy to lead the stray sheep back to the fold, while giving witness to the rest of the flock that there are grave consequences when one acts against the teachings of the Church. If you said nothing, if you were silent, you are among the bishops who love the sin, and in reality, do not love the sinner. You hate him; otherwise, you would confront him publicly. This will not be excused at your judgment before God, unless you change now and speak out.

A great bishop made cardinal—
Cardinal Robert Sarah states:

"It is a serious responsibility for every bishop to be and to represent the mind of Christ. Bishops who scatter the sheep that Jesus has entrusted to them will be judged mercilessly and severely by God."[12]

Cardinal R. Sarah

Even a first grader knows to hate the sin and love the sinner. You bishops, with all the letters of your degrees behind your name, to show how highly intelligent and educated you are, only show us, peasants in the pew, that you have been indoctrinated with the poison of intellectualism. Our Lady of Medjugorje said:

December 2, 2007

> **"…God's Word…is the … light of common sense."**

Never, in almost 40 years, has Our Lady praised intellectualism.

*"Thank you, thank you, thank you! You have
called a spade a spade and rightfully so! I
will continue to pray for the bishops that they
will be moved to action by the Holy Spirit
as you have been all these years! Biden &
Pelosi MUST be excommunicated! So many
in the pews see this, yet the bishops refuse
to use the power given to them by Almighty
God! I pray they heed this message! YOU,
and a few holy priests, are what has kept me
faithful to the Catholic faith all these years! I
have longed for the Church of my youth, and
a world where morality and truth within the
Church were what convicted sinners. When
we lost that, we lost the ability to see our
own sins. Bishops included! God has given
his Mother to us and She has given You to
us! God Bless you, your family and the Community of Caritas!"*

Julie
Fredericksburg, TX

CHAPTER EIGHT

The Failing of our Shepherds

Our Lady has been teaching and guiding hundreds of millions across the world with Her messages for almost 40 years and not once has the United States Conference of Catholic Bishops given a word to help propagate Her plans and instructions, that will save the whole world, bringing the world to conversion. Our Lady said:

June 25, 2007

> **"... Little children, do not forget that
> you are all important in this great plan,
> which God leads through Medjugorje.
> God desires to convert the entire
> world and to call it to salvation and to
> the way towards Himself, who is the**

**beginning and the end of every being.
In a special way, little children, from
the depth of my heart, I call you all to
open yourselves to this great grace that
God gives you through my presence
here..."**

In order to stop satan from destroying the world,
Our Lady, for years, has been saying:

March 18, 2009

**"...Do not forget your shepherds. Pray
that they <u>may not get lost</u>, that they
may remain in my Son so as to be good
shepherds to their flock..."**

If the bishops were not lost, would there be any
reason to pray for them not to get lost?

May 2, 2011

**"...I am especially praying for the
shepherds, for God <u>to help them to</u>**

be alongside you with a fullness of heart…"

You don't have to help shepherds to be alongside their flock with fullness of heart unless they *are not* alongside us, with fullness of heart. I have been through five different bishops while growing the largest Medjugorje mission in the world, producing millions of books and pieces of materials about Medjugorje. After one particular meeting with my third bishop, I asked him for a blessing. He refused the blessing. When I asked him why, he responded, *"I don't know how you will use it."* Thirty days later, I was in the Vatican with Pope John Paul II discussing Medjugorje, my mission, the Caritas community and our life. Without asking, the Holy Father gave me a blessing with his thumb on my forehead. He then put his hands on my head in a second blessing for my family. I knelt down before him and he blessed me, with his arms stretched out, a third time for the community. Pope John Paul

II was spiritually awake. He didn't ask me how I would use his blessing. He understood the conversion of our work. This is exactly what this writing is about—to awake what is asleep in the bishops and, thereby, wake up the parishes to massive conversion.

September 2, 2011

> **"...I am especially praying for the shepherds that they <u>may be worthy</u> representatives of my Son..."**

Bishops, are you worthy representatives of Our Lady's Son? If you are, why does Our Lady say, **"I'm praying for you that you <u>may be</u> worthy?"**

July 2, 2016

> **"...I implore you to pray a lot for your shepherds, to pray so as to have all the more love for them because my Son gave them to you...Therefore, also you**

are to love them. But, my children, remember, <u>love means to endure</u> and to give, and never, ever to judge…"

Yes, Our Lady said never, ever to judge you. That was stated at the beginning of this writing. Your judgement is reserved only for God. If we, the peasants living Our Lady's messages, refrain from your judgement, what is stated here is to spotlight how and why you are off track and to state to you what we need. You have failed the flock and the Holy Virgin Mary's plans brought here by the Queen of Peace.

"WOW! This is AWESOME! Yes I am copying and sending this to my local cardinal, former President of the USCCB. Now is the time, backed by Our Lady, through much, much prayer, penance, fasting and Her messages, to show moral courage. No matter what! Thank you, Caritas and Terry Colafrancesco, for your faithful witness and convictions in this our great time of need! Thank you for your witness and tirelessly getting out those great messages. I am now clinging to them like a life preserver and through the Holy Rosary am now beginning to find peace amid sooo much confusion...What does a faithful Catholic do, where do I go, when even some of my...Catholic friends and my family, to seem to just lay down, lick their wounds, roll over and say, 'Well, it's God's Will.' Let's obey, put our mask on and go along to get along hoping and praying for better times. Our Lady's messages say different, as does this writing. Thanks for giving this poor soul a sense of direction and soo much peace and joy! I am not afraid of whatever the future holds because in the end, 'Mary's Immaculate Heart Will Triumph.' God's love to Caritas, Our Lady's First Apostles"

L.S.

Houston, TX

CHAPTER NINE

Man Up

As bishops, you have also fallen for satan's building oneness through centralization. Centralization amalgamates both the Light and the dark together. Globalization is the goal, both in the state and in the Church. It is a diabolical plan that will institute a universal, minimal income for everyone, no private property, a new capitalism where governments go away, and "corporate capitalism" prevails. It is not a free market. Law will give way to regulations, standardized across the world. Globalism is a perfect incubator to birth an antichrist system. Many in the Church hierarchy have bought into it. The world governments have bought into it. Our Lady is here to dismantle it. And you fall for it.

Centralization, at this moment, gives great power to few and does not distinguish between Light and dark. Light, therefore, is eclipsed and darkness prevails. God, on the contrary, separates the Light vs. the dark for unity. How unity? Light will draw many to the Light, ***"seeing how they love one another."*** The USCCB shines light upon "the Bidens"—bringing no one to conversion. All the while the peasants in the pew grow more discontent. Go ahead and have your stupid meetings while the peasants are starving to death from a lack of spiritual food. Having pity for the sheep, Jesus sends His Mother with all the answers needed, but you, instead, smother Her plans with your own plans and proclamations that don't work. We don't need any more conferences. We need real men. Man Up. Stand Up. We do not need calmed-down eunuchs. Are you offended by this? Then prove it to be a false statement. A real bishop would not be offended, with a girly attitude, *"I am so offended."*

He would be convicted. That is what you need—conviction. For example, we need men willing to forget a stupid position of being "nuanced" towards elections when it is clear that Biden is a bad actor, a very bad actor. Just shout it out. Watch the flock, flock around you! Will you? Many have lost hope in you, but not in Our Lady.

Bishops, your greatest sin is that you have rejected Our Lady's plans to save us from the prevailing darkness we are now experiencing. Many of you, who have been at the helm of the Church these almost 40 years, have been there for at least some period of Our Lady's apparitions. Every square inch of the world is under a jurisdiction of a diocese, underneath the authority of a bishop. For four decades, the world has denigrated into a boiling cauldron of stench under your watch, as already said, but necessary to repeat. Your answer is to meet at a conference to talk and eat, talk and eat, talk and eat. Are you fasting on bread and water twice a week as Our Lady said **is necessary?** Are you doing nine-day bread and water fasts several times a year? We, in our Community, do so. We have our adolescents, even our children, participate with no complaining, but with joy! (Yes, nine days!) Are you praying three hours a day? Many across the world are doing this because Our Lady said we must fast on bread and water at least two times weekly and pray three hours every day.

A warning to you bishops of the United States and of the world: You are going to enter into a most severe depth of inescapable lamentation that many of you will wish you were dead. Why? Because you will come to know, through the first three Secrets from God, foretold by the Virgin Mary of Medjugorje over these almost 40 years, that Our Lady was truly present in the world and you did not accept Her. These Secrets are coming soon. How many millions of souls were sent to perdition, that could have been saved if you had listened these four decades to what Our Lady has been saying and declared: *"My diocese is open to the Queen of Peace. Propagate Her messages."*

Our Lady's words, have been telling the people of the world, **"listen to me, I will teach you."** If you, as bishops, ordered every parish in your diocese to open to Medjugorje, for every Catholic school to open to Medjugorje, and for every Catholic university and institution to open to Medjugorje, you would experience and see a natural grace, a tsunami flood of conversion over your diocese that will bloom in a way you cannot imagine. But no, your indifference, your tokenism of Our Lady's apparitions, putting the USCCB's agendas over God's plans to save the world has prevailed. Surrounded by the curtains of power that control you and keep you in fear, you allow the killing of Our Lady's plans. You blind yourselves from the reality that is right in front of you.

For examplc, in 2011, it was reported that there were **<u>106 Catholic colleges/institutions</u>** that

were *"abominable lifestyle sin friendly."* These
universities promote and protect abominable relationships and perverted false unions masked as
marriage as in Sodom. These colleges/institutions
are in your dioceses. Are you guilty of hiding behind the argument, *"Well, its under another religious
orders jurisdiction?"* They are in your diocese!
Man up. Shut them down or strip "Catholic" from
their names and make your judgement known. This
anti-Catholic ideology is rampant on our Catholic
university campuses. You cannot use the excuse, *"I
didn't know that."* Then how do I, a layman, know
it? Get rid of the curtain of power around you and
don't listen to them. You run the diocese, not others. Build a research team outside of your office to
feed you truth. If you do not escape the curtains of
power around you, and those who want to climb the
ladder, you will not thrive. Get out of the bishop
conferences. Run your diocese with the boldness of
Jesus. Say what you know you have to say.

"Extraordinary!!! Brave and clear as it is, will print it and go to my bishop to give him a copy. If he does not speak English, will offer him to translate in any form that would be needed. We must stop being cowards and letting our shepherds to be so!!! This false pandemic is taking so many out of discernment and Our Lady's messages are needed more than ever to convict and covert. Thanks a lot to a Friend of Medjugorje for this writing."

B.S.
Mexico

70

CHAPTER TEN

Change Your Course

The USCCB's agendas are riddled with what
and why the Church is in decline. You won't open
to Medjugorje, but you let Socialism and Communism, prosper within the Church. If you do not
understand that sentence, *"Socialism and Communism in the Church,"* you are reading the wrong
books and listening to the wrong people, such as
the Maryknoll Missionaries who propagate "socialist justice" in their magazines that can be found
in many diocesan offices and waiting areas. The
Maryknoll Missionaries have, for many decades,
openly and shamefully defended and encouraged
in the Church, Communist and Socialist mentalities
and philosophies, teaching "victimization" instead

of what Jesus taught in how to win over your op-
pressors.

As to the Maryknoll Missionaries, you bishops lend support to them simply by your silence, as
well as allowing their magazines in diocesan offices and churches. But no Medjugorje information
can be in your offices and churches. In fact, God
forbid if Medjugorje material is found in the parishes, which God has not forbidden; but you have
by your indifference, silenced or outright banned
it. All the while, Our Lady of Medjugorje has requested, for nearly 40 years, to spread Her messages
to everyone. This is far more scandalous than the
great scandal of abomination that has entered and
plagued the Church for the past two decades. We
don't want to hear any more about Cardinal Mc-
Carrick. **Quit the PR of *"look at us, we are transparent."*** Stop bringing it up. It is nauseating. Move
on. Move on to Our Lady, to Medjugorje. Leave
what is trash in the garbage can. If you had opened

to Our Lady, She would have swept clean the mess you allowed. It would have been gone a long time ago because Our Lady came on the daily scene in 1981 warning you.

August 29, 1982

Concerning reports that **"the apparitions"** have divided the priests in Hercegovina (Medjugorje):

> **"I have not desired your division. On the contrary, I desire that you be united. <u>Do not 'ignore'</u> the fact that I am the Queen of Peace. If you desire practical advice: I am the Mother <u>who has come from the people</u>; I cannot do anything without the help of God. I, too, must pray like you. It is because of that, that I can only say to you: Pray, fast, do penance, and help the weak. I am sorry if my preceding answer was**

**not agreeable to you. Perhaps you do
not want to understand it."**

This writing about what future awaits you,
bishops, is not to condemn you, but to convict you.
You have but a very short time to change your
course by choosing to open every parish, school and
Catholic institution in your dioceses to the Queen
of Peace, Her messages and Her plans to save the
world or be prepared for martyrdom, each and every one of you. Our Lady said:

December 2, 2015

> **"…it is necessary to pray much, to
> pray and love the Church to which
> you belong. Now, the Church <u>is suffer-
> ing</u> and needs apostles …The Church
> needs apostles, who by living the Eu-
> charist with the heart, <u>do great works</u>;
> it needs you, my apostles…From the
> very beginning, the Church was per-**

secuted and betrayed, but day by day it grew. It is indestructible... Pray for your shepherds <u>that they may have the strength</u>...to be bridges of salvation...

"...that they may have strength..." Stop for a moment. Think. Reflect. Contemplate these words. If the shepherds, who are the apostles, had strength, if they were **"bridges of salvation,"** then why would Our Lady say the Church is suffering and needs apostles? Again, Our Lady follows, saying again:

"The Church needs apostles...to do great works..."

Then Our Lady says, **"...it needs you..."**

Then Our Lady says **"...you,..."** saying **"...my apostles..."**

referencing the laity, the peasants in the pews,

which means the apostolic apostles, the shepherds, are not doing the job of being **"...bridges of salvation..."**

Therefore, Our Lady is here to raise up a body of apostles from the laity to rebuild the Church, as St. Louis de Montfort prophesied. The bishops have failed. Forty years have almost passed since the first apparitions of Our Lady in Medjugorje. Many bishops recognize the major magnitude of the six apparitions of Fatima, and yet have not grasped that every day, an apparition on the scale of a Fatima apparition is taking place in Medjugorje. It is not even put in second place, but way down the pole of importance. Your attitude of nonbelief, nonchalant and noncommittal indifference is all to your demise. You cannot and will not get that time back. Again, how many went to hell in these decades because you didn't give them the medicine from Heaven that would have healed their souls instead of the spiritual diseases that sent them to hell? Will you be judged with severity by God, mercilessly, as Cardinal Sarah said and which merits to be repeated:

> *"It is a serious responsibility for every bishop to be and to represent the mind of Christ. Bishops who scatter the sheep that Jesus has entrusted to them will be judged mercilessly and severely by God."[13]*

"Everything I read is 1000% true. God help our shepherds. They want to be popular among the people rather than say it like it is. Sin is sin, no matter how you slice it."

J.L.

Knoxville, TN

CHAPTER ELEVEN

Freedom to Propagate

I'm a "podunk" ditch digger with an education, qualified by the following letters behind my name: 72 D's, 13 F's, and flunked third grade, yet have been educated 38 years through the Queen of Peace School of Medjugorje, but I speak of your lethargic, pathetic indifference, your incompetence as Christ's apostles, lovers of the robes and of the limelight, prideful men who misuse your power, or do not use your power for good. Do you grade yourselves through the covering of the USCCB with a grade A+? Are these words too harsh? This is an observation of almost 40 years of study, of looking for you to act and, yet, you do nothing but let the Church suffer and decline under you.

Yes, there are some good bishops, but they are an endangered species. And yet, they have not gone all out to explode Medjugorje's Queen of Peace and Her messages throughout every corner of their diocese. How do we know a good bishop? He is one who listens to Heaven, when Heaven is speaking. If you consider yourself a good bishop, don't interfere or even try to define Medjugorje. Just let it open up with a super green light in your dioceses. Give it freedom to propagate. Our Lady will guide it. Watch the explosion of conversions and the loyalty that will grow towards you and towards your office. It will literally explode as well. Along with a great many conversions. But, **BEWARE** and be ready for division and the attack from satan on every parish. I state it will happen. Why? Because Our Lady said:

January 28, 1987

"…Whenever I come to you my Son comes with me, but so does satan…"

Again, we do not judge you. Our Lady made it clear that Jesus would judge you, just as Cardinal Sarah stated. Our Lady said:

March 2, 2019

> **"…I am calling you to mercy…I am imploring you, my children, to forgive…"**

I and all the peasants in the pew forgive you and we pray for mercy for you, because when you wake up, you will have realized, in great horror, that you missed the time of Mary. Our Lady said:

August 25, 2013

> **"…I do not desire for you, dear children, to have to repent for everything that you could have done but did not want to…"**

Bishops, remember what David Barton stated about "the cowards and the fearful." He said, this is the first group that God sends to hell because of what they didn't do. (Revelation 21:8) Medjugorje is running out of time. It's time to lift all the restrictions that suppress Medjugorje. Is Medjugorje approved. Yes, 100%. Medjugorje is believed by hundreds of millions of people who have been profoundly converted, and who have changed their lives for the better. It is approved by the people scattered across the whole world, ***Sensus Fidelium***. No more debate.

Queen of Peace,
Save Our Nation and Her People,

Friend of Medjugorje

Friend of Medjugorje

A Declaration for Public Record

January 18, 2021

The following signers have read what is stated, and by signing or going on record and are testifying to their 100% agreement, alignment and sentiments in regard to what a Friend of Medjugorje has written to you; the failures of the bishops and the USCCB and all bishops' conferences across the world. You, bishops, must take the above to heart and must release the peasants in the pew to propagate Our Lady of Medjugorje. There can be no more waiting to spread Our Lady's messages and plans.

1. Tony Colafrancesco — Community of Caritas
2. Erin Colafrancesco — Community of Caritas
3. Faith Colafrancesco — Community of Caritas
4. Victoria Colafrancesco — Community of Caritas
5. Ruth McDonald — Community of Caritas
6. Joan McDonald — Community of Caritas

7.   Jessica Ross—Community of Caritas
8.   Reyes Silva—Community of Caritas
9.   Jason Terrell—Community of Caritas
10. Zachary Doctor—Community of Caritas
11. Austin Blanchard—Community of Caritas
12. Jeff Pipp—Community of Caritas
13. Robin Pipp—Community of Caritas
14. Steve Fabian—Community of Caritas
15. Kathy Fabian—Community of Caritas
16. Will Uhlenhake—Community of Caritas
17. Patty Uhlenhake—Community of Caritas
18. Jacinta Uhlenhake—Community of Caritas
19. Joy Uhlenhake—Community of Caritas
20. Anne Uhlenhake—Community of Caritas
21. Mary Uhlenhake—Community of Caritas
22. Angela Uhlenhake—Community of Caritas
23. Martha Uhlenhake—Community of Caritas
24. Joe Hudachek—Community of Caritas
25. Jenny Hudachek—Community of Caritas
26. Dan Jackson—Community of Caritas
27. Annabelle Orichefsky—Community of Caritas
28. Christopher Antone—Community of Caritas
29. Michael Capelle—Extended Community of Caritas
30. Michael Pater—Berwick, Victoria, Australia
31. Eduardo Fraga—Miami, FL
32. Marvalee—Maricopa, AZ
33. Jeanette A. Coury—Houston, TX
34. Alan Eckl—Florence, AL
35. Maria Eckl—Florence, AL

36. Linda Marie Prince — Wilmington, DE
37. Douglas Bourbina — Bloomington, IN
38. Jerinel Maynard — Dublin, OH
39. Maureen Murphy — Madison, MS
40. June Downey — Grant Park, IL
41. Donald Wires — Loveland, OH
42. Bridgette Barnhart — Saint Louis, MO
43. Frances Bigeni — Central Coast, Australia
44. Jihane Allen — Okotoks, Alberta, Canada
45. Robert McLeer — Lawrenceville, GA
46. Art Zavala — Anaheim, CA
47. Patty Morales — Humble, TX
48. Georgene Brook — Redmond, OR
49. Barbara Wilson — Boerne, TX
50. Francine Amy — Vero Beach, FL
51. Regina McMahon — Cochranville, PA
52. Elvira Lowe — Woodbridge, VA
53. Cathy Tharp — Bardstown, KY
54. Connie Thomas — Harwood, TX
55. Dan Kremer — Yorkshire, OH
56. Mary Boyce — Eufaula, AL
57. Lisa Evans — Marysville, WA
58. Gene Velasquez — Chimayo, NM
59. Luci Holloway — Port Townsend, WA
60. James Snodgrass — Macomb, MI
61. Maritza Romero — Modesto, CA
62. Nichole Schmidt — Celina, OH
63. Eugene Morales — Humble, TX
64. Laura Miller — Breaux Bridge, LA

65. Rachelle Blackman—Deland, FL

66. Leonard Long—Galloway, NJ

67. Marie Ram—Chino Hills, CA

68. Marge Barton—Fenton, MO

69. Jodie Faltysek—East Bernard, TX

70. Jeri Gumerson—Greenwood, IN

71. Daniel Kortes—New Baltimore, MI

72. Jackie Ramnarong—Fort Wayne, IN

73. Sherry Hittle—Ida Grove, IA

74. Teresa Thompson—Rock Hill, SC

75. Peggy Wojcik—Columbus, NE

76. Susan—Conway, CA

77. Dee Logsdon—Springfield, KY

78. Janice Hirsch—Odell, IL

79. Deb—Romeoville, IL

80. Mary Rausser—Somers, NY

81. Lois Opincar—Avon Lake, OH

82. Kathy Winner—Minster, OH

83. Carolyn Montenegro—Hopewell Junction, NY

84. Mychelle Davis—Ellijay, GA

85. Jill Finkenbine—Maplewood, OH

86. Kamanzi May Faustina—Kampala,Uganda, Africa

87. Monica Vigil—Espanola, NM

88. Peggy Gleason—Shakopee, MN

89. Cynthia Gabaldon,—La Verne, CA

90. Barbara Heizmann—Oak Hill, FL

91. Ann Willenbring—Richmond, MN

92. Margaret Grossman—Benson, MN

93. Susana G. Fullerton—Kents Store, VA

94. Sharon Allende—Fountain Valley, CA
95. Barbara Heagy — Milton, DE
96. Kathie Jackson—Tulsa, OK
97. Donna Cummings—Mechanicsville, IA
98. Janice Tidmarsh—Cave Creek, AZ
99. Pam Coulon—Gonzales, LA
100. Maureen Ann Redler—Decatur, AL
101. Cynthia—Edinburg, TX
102. Jacqueline Robinson—Barrie, Ontario Canada
103. Margaret Solimene—East Hartford, CT
104. Steve Craig—Orange Grove, TX
105. Delores Cook -Barnesville, MN
106. Eileen Fusaro—Wappingers Fall, NY
107. Nora Zurek—Clarkston, MI
108. Joanne Mento—Newtown Square, PA

This list is just the names we had at the time of the first printing. Many people are sending their names in, and they will be included in the next printing of this book. **It is time to stand up and let our names be shown.** Mail in your name to Caritas of Birmingham or sign up on medjugorje.com to be included in this list of signers. We will be updating this list on a regular basis.

"I'm worried about my judgment day for trans-gressions that I was not aware are sins. How much more the bishops should be worried, they have received all the teachings of Jesus!! Those of whom much is given, much is expected. I hope that this writing is sent to ALL the bish-ops in the USA. They have failed us miserably. May God have mercy on them. I will print this out and send to my bishop and it will prob-ably be read by a subordinate and then thrown away. I might believe them when they divest of all their trappings, especially certain cardinals of which I am thinking. No more platitudes. DO SOMETHING CONCRETE. Stop pillorying our beloved priests who do speak out!…I could say more but I would just get 'worked up' all the more and a Friend of Medjugorje says it much better than me. May Jesus have mercy on us! Our Lady Queen of Peace, pray for us."

Mary
Paso Robles, California

Testimonies

The following are testimonies that we have received from all over the world, for people who have read *Blind to Your Wrong*. We wanted to share them with you, so that you can see how much this book has effected others.

"I am a cradle Catholic although like some, I was not schooled in Catholic school beyond third grade. I was, however educated by my grandparents in the Catholic faith. There was never any hesitation, in telling us 'young people,' what was demanded, required or expected from us with regards to our moral behavior, in our Catholic faith. It came to Life in my teens…being in high school in the '60s There was an Explosion of Freedom. If it makes you happy do it; It's my body, no one can tell me what to do with it. Teachers hands were tied as far as discipline went and disposable marriages the norm rather than the rarity. Despite this onslaught of confusion our Catholic faith was our foundation. Our Strength. Our Security. Unchanged. WE WANT THIS BACK! The laws based on Our God-given 10 Commandments. One Nation Under God, Indivisible with Liberty and Justice for All."

Fay Rome

"Thank you from the bottom of my heart for your courage in standing up to these men. It gives me the courage to be more bold in my faith. Bless you."

R.Q.
Saratoga Springs, NY

"Thank you, Friend of Medjugorje! My husband and I have been wrestling with this for quite some time. Now more than ever, we have been seeing greater signs of complacency and indifference. When I recently asked a priest why we are not hearing more from the pulpit, in regard to moral issues, the pope's opposite teachings and examples, etc., I was told that Pope Francis says that the homilies need to focus on the Gospel and bringing the people peace. Also, I was told that they have to be careful on how they approach moral matters. Why? They were not careful telling me the truth when I was being educated. Like it or not, the truth was told and morals were clearly defined. Your writing is with accuracy and aligns with what my husband and I have been seeing. With the complacency at hand, we are now dealing with a much bigger mess. Truth needs to be clearly revealed NOW. There is no reason to pacify the pope's erroneous teachings (nor anyone else). Truth does not sway; it must be told with vigor! It must be followed by Biblical teachings, by the One True Doctrine of Faith! We pray for God's mercy to be upon us and for many conversions to take place. We pray for our shepherds and for clarity in truth—for our eyes and ears to be opened, the fog removed leaving only the One True Faith! We pray for them to lead us on the path of righteousness via the Bible's teachings. Our Lady reaffirms this in Her messages. As you have mentioned before that *if Our Lady of Medjugorje is the last stop, we do not have time to evaluate it before the period of Grace is over and the critical nature of the messages are upon us. What will this hurt??? Obviously, there is so much evidence (even agreed by scientists, in regard to the supernatural involvement); there is so much love, peace and conversion. The enemy is at hand and we must carefully discern. However, by now, we can see that the enemy can not bring such peace and love as has been bestowed upon the people via Our Lady and Her messages in Medjugorje. If this is of God, it will not leave us; however, the time of Grace is upon us and will not be here forever. And so far, 40 years have remained. Let us not ignore Our Lord and Our Lady any further. We can plainly see that not acknowledging it for what it is has certainly kept our country from being a better place, not to mention the salvation of souls that could have transpired. Let us not wait any longer. May the Divine Intervention of Our Lord and Our Lady be upon us! God bless you all and thank you for your love and genuine commitment to Our Lord and Our Lady!"*

C.B.

Cincinnati, OH

"May we see the true light you have given us and awaken the people to the lies of leaders and corrupt doing so much harm to people and the Nation. Praying in small groups and Holy Hours before the blessed Sacrament and we are getting converts as very good lay people helping to convert. God bless and have Mercy on the USA and end murder of our unborn and have respect for life again. Thank you for all the truthful information."

M.A.K.

Cottonwood, ID

"Eloquently written! Two sets of books! I.e. two versions of the Twelve Commandments? First version for the peasant flock. Second version for the Church hierarchy and politicians."

Ron

Santa Clara, CA

"A reminder to all us peasants in the pews who have been to Medjugorje...We must live the messages and bring Medjugorje HERE!!!! God bless you, and the Caritas Community, for speaking TRUTH and witnessing to all with your lives."

J.J.

Woodbury, MN

"Extraordinary piece. I was happy to see that the bishops responded by criticizing Biden, but until they act it's only words. The bishops unfortunately aren't the only ones that are guilty. So is the head of the Catholic Church, our pope. May God hear the prayers of the faithful and may Our Lady continue to help us."

Linda

Joliet, IL

"Thank you for always speaking the truth. Our nation is certainly in a very bad spot as most Catholics believe what is "preached" to them instead of what is Divinely inspired in them as truth. It is a sad day for our nation that we have to endure Joe Biden's presidency and all the harm that it will bring, but with your voice out there we will have a beacon of light to follow. May God bless you and everyone at Caritas for putting your lives on notice for all of us."

L.G.

Rochester, NY

"It is truly a shame that our bishops and Church did not educate their flock about their responsibility as Catholics to vote in accordance with Jesus' teaching and Church teachings. A few in my extended family voted for Biden and I was unable to convince them otherwise because they had been indoctrinated by the media and untruths spoken in our culture. If the priests and bishops had done their job and guided the flock, many would have voted responsibly but silence gave permission to vote for Biden. And the silence continues to allow him to "act" like a Catholic, attend mass and receive Communion. He and the other people in high office should be excommunicated without hesitation. They are a disgrace to the Catholic faith. Thank God we have a Friend of Medjugorje to give all of us a voice and speak what we hold in our hearts. We must continue this message and share with all we know. We are so grateful to have our Holy Mother with us to teach us and guide us. Let us pray as She says for the shepherds. We need them to hear us and lead us. Thank you, Friend of Medjugorje and God bless you and the community."

LW.

Houston, TX

"While reading this and based on the 'Friend of Medjugorje's' proclamation that he is not a highly educated man, It is inconceivable to not be aware that the Holy Spirit wrote these words through him. The eloquence of this statement is sublime (and long overdue)."

M.H.

Cedar Rapids, IA

"My wife and I are very strong Conservatives and strong believers in the Catholic Church. We have followed the visionaries since the 90's because of a Friend of Medjugorje.

"We were very disappointed with our Catholic bishops supporting President Biden, knowing how he feels about abortion and certain marriages. For Biden to want unity in America and killing 11,000 jobs on Day 1 was insane, un-American. He has already signed over 25 Executive Orders in two days. We pray for Biden to wake up before America destroys itself. May God have mercy on us. God bless a Friend of Medjugorje and Caritas. Stay strong."

J.G.

New Deal, TX

"Amen!"

B.

Argos, IN

"Praise be Jesus! It is about time someone stood up and said it like it is. May God bless you. Mother pray for us."

M.R.

Lubbock, TX

"It breaks my heart so much to know that there is now a President in the White House who hates the gift of God's babies. I try to do as much as I can to help the little ones by praying for them, signing petitions and helping friends who want an abortion. I hate the word and would happily do what I could, in excess of what I have already done, if it were possible. If I lived in America it might be easier but

where I live it is more difficult. I just know it breaks my heart now that Trump has left and the babies no longer have a champion. They have a killer in the White House now!"

J.

North Hamptonshire, UK

"Beautifully written. Prayer and fasting, as requested by our Blessed Mother, will be our salvation if we only follow Her requests. I have been to Medjugorje twice, and have been blessed to have been present during two apparitions. Highlights of my life. This is the eleventh hour, and it is now or never for the conversion of souls. The bishops need to lead their flocks. We, the believers, will support them when they follow God's Commandments. Do not be afraid. Lead by example. Many will follow."

S.M.

Rancho Cucamonga, CA

"Ever notice that those with the courage to give a STRONG homily—are the RETIRED PRIESTS, filling in for a pastor. They no longer fear the feedback of those upset by THE TRUTH! For some reason I have admired COURAGE! The courage of 'Students for Life,' a good example ,whom I donate to and thank God for!! I have found that you need to Pray 'ASK THE HOLY SPIRIT' for the courage - to do God's Will for you !!!"

D.P.

Frazee, MN

"Right on. The Bishops should tell their sheep Joe Biden & Nancy Pelosi are excommunicated from the Catholic Church. In 1991, I visited Medjugorje and returned to Church after being away for 15 years. What is wrong with these bishops!!"

P.B.

Wakefield, MA

"Decades of discernment as clear as day and the fruit of prayer and fasting. Truth is Truth and Light is Light. This is not just a USA problem. Thank you for your strength and leadership. God bless the Community of Caritas."

Eric

Scotland

"Thank you for such a justified upbraiding. We should have taken these men to task years ago. Biden has just refunded International Planned Parenthood, and committed our tax dollars to pay for it. satan has surely taken over control of our country, but we both know that God is stronger than satan. Thank you for giving the bishops fodder to chew and I hope and pray that they accept this as positive feedback that they have earned. May God have mercy on them. Now I understand much better why our Churches are losing membership and financial support. May God bless you and the family of Caritas."

Larry

Grand Rapids, MI

"If I were a bishop, I'd sure take another look at my actions (or inaction) and consider immediate changes. Well done and well expressed.

Even I understood all of it. Our Lady must be happy with you as Her Apostle. Biden has now reversed President Trump's protections against abortion and is making taxpayers pay the cost. God help us. I've set on Church boards several times, charged with the task of determining the cause of people leaving the Church and not contributing financially or morally toward the welfare of the Church. You've opened my eyes and I feel more prepared for the future if I'm ever asked to sit on a board again. God bless you, and the family of Caritas."

Larry

Grand Rapids, MI

"Great writing! Exactly to the point! Fasting and praying for all shepherds. Thank you, a Friend of Medjugorje and Caritas Community for all you do for Our Lady of Medjugorje Queen of Peace."

F.R.

Cleveland, TX.

"I wanted to cheer and shout. Exactly what they need to hear. I am waiting for action from them. I am so tired of hearing about their meetings that mean nothing to us. So we'll spoken. Thank you. Lead us on, I cannot wait."

E.H.

Grand Idle, LA

"Thank you once again, and again, and yet again, for your inspired writings. 'Way back about 1960 (when I spent a few years in a Catholic seminary) the prophetic word was making the rounds that 'the time of the laity was upon us' and the standard (deliberately innocu-

ous) interpretation given was that the laity was then to be given more activity in ecclesiastical functions (this because at that day it was very true that most lay people left everything up to the clergy, even Catholic education of children). We all know about what the ever-present satanic influence did to this concept (for only one example, extraordinary ministers of the Eucharist); in fact, I have seen this concept in print in a church document as 'extra ordinary ministers' and I still see priests sitting down or standing behind the altar while others distribute the Eucharist. OK. We are where we are. But back to the prophetic word: I myself did not realize at the time that what was actually meant and prophetic was that the majority of the Catholic clergy would soon come to abdicate their responsibilities, and that Our Lady would be right there to fill up the gap by using the peons in the pews. It's time to put my name and address on the line as being 120% behind this writing."

Murph

Milton-Freewater, OR

"Nice going Terry sounds like truth to me especially the part that struck me they never opened up the Churches to our Lady of Medjugorje! Praise be to Jesus, Our Lady Queen of Peace be with us protect us and pray for us. Thank you for your Fiat."

M.B.

Mithtown, NY

"At Mass last weekend, the priest, who is traditional and one of two beautiful priests at our parish in Baton Rouge, read the 'Prayer for Our Government' written in 1791 by the first bishop in America,

100

Bishop John Carroll, whose prayer to God was to endow the gifts of the Holy Spirit on our government and government leaders. Immediately following that prayer from Bishop John Carroll, the priest read a letter written by our Bishop of Baton Rouge to all Church parishes, reinforcing the use of face masks and social distancing!!! I exclaimed out loud 'What a contrast!' Where are our shepherds, O Lord?"

Marie

Baton Rouge, LA

"Yes, a fire needs to be set!! Mary has come to quiet us with the WORD of GOD!!"

G.W.

Sooke, British Columbia, Canada

"Thank you, Queen Virgin Mother, for giving AFOM the grace to speak and witness the TRUTH of the HOLY TRINITY."

F.V.

Abbeville, LA

"An amazing piece. I learned so much from this writing. It saddened me when New York passed the late-term abortion law and the law makers stood and applauded with not retribution from the Church. Also, when California passed laws favorable to pedophiles with the Church remaining silent. All I could think of was Sodom and Gomorrah right here in our country."

Janice

Odell, IL

"THANK YOU! I felt like getting up and cheering that someone finally said it as it is. I hope and pray that Our Lady cleans out the hierarchy... they are doing such a disservice to the flock. Their duplicity and 'nuanced' approach is sickening. So thank you for clearly stating the truth. May Our Lady and Our Lord bless you and keep you and give you peace, and give us wisdom and peace as we fight the good fight - without our bishops. THEY are the problem!!!"

K.M.

"I could not believe that our bishops had gone so low until a friend sent me this Facebook message from Bishop John Stowe this afternoon. I was sick at heart. To speak about My Biden as a noble and honorable man when he promotes abortion and [abominable] marriages, it's hypocrisy!!! He goes against everything our Church believes! He promotes sin against the people, the Commandments, against God!! I am worried for our Church, for our nation, for the souls of our leaders!!!"

Vicki

St. Charles, MO

"I just went to Confession on Saturday and I Confessed to our priest that I am currently helping my daughter. She has to live with me at the moment, but she brought her fiance because they had nowhere to live (they lost their jobs). I wanted to Confess my part in contributing to their mortal sin. The priest told me that it was OK because this is the culture! I asked, 'But does GOD say this is ok?' I totally see what AFOM is saying. I am so grateful that my mother visited Medjugorje years ago. I am new to this website and group, but I am

learning so much. I plan to print this and give it to our bishop and priest. I printed the previous writings from AFOM and gave my priest the book <u>They Fired the First Shot</u>. *I really hope he reads it."*

M.B.

Beaumont, TX

"God Bless you FOM. A true message of love and a convicting message. Reminds me of many of Our Lady's messages. (September 2, 2013)"

T.S.

Fort Loramie, OH

Yes, the Church hierarchy has failed us. With the prophesies from Fatima and with Medjugorje. I see a revival in other Christian denominations, but not here in our Catholic Church. Our flock lacks leadership. As Mother Mary continues to tell us pray, pray, pray."

Tom

Belmont, NH

We have followed Our Lady's Messages from the beginning and have presented ourselves in Medjugorje. With a strong and fervent belief in Her Messages our lives have been changed. We, too, are disgusted and dismayed at the lack of leadership from our Bishops and Cardinals. Our fervent, daily prayer is for the conversion of hearts, salvation of souls, and an end to the lukewarmness which exists in our Church and its members. May god have Mercy on us and our country!

F.K.D.

Wheaton, IL

Dear A Friend of Medjugorje,

"This is a must read for all the bishops with little time that is left and that they may change their course of direction to allow Our Lady to help bring about many souls to conversions. Your conviction and the truth of this writing should be an eye-opener for majority of the bishops who needs to be spiritually awaken. We, the sheep in the pews, are demanding for a change to remove all darkness and false conflicting actions by your inactions and by our sinful ways we have allowed darkness to infiltrate the Church. We continue to pray for you in hopes you heed the warnings. We are all sinners, no judgment, but only pleas, for many souls are at stake. Let Our Lady guide us all!

"Thank you, A Friend of Medjugorje (Community of Caritas and Birmingham), for living Our Lady's messages and helping us all along the way to strive to live and imitate into our way of living. We love Our Lady and Mother and give ourselves under Her care to be Her extended hands. Glory and thanks be to God in this time of Grace by Her presence and guidance. Thank you, Blessed Mother, for guiding us for 40 years! May God bless us all!"

With Love and Prayers,
C.C. of Texas

"God bless you Friend of Medjugorje and the Community of Caritas. Tirelessly, you work, pray unceasingly, and strictly fast according to Our Lady's instructions. Our shepherds' fasts are a joke in compari-son. I am so grateful and thankful for your presence in my life. O Mary, conceived without sin, pray for us who have recourse to You. I surrender myself and my will to Jesus, my Lord & Savior. I have

much to atone for but with God's guidance, the Sacrament of Reconciliation, and the Eucharist, I will be armed with the resolve to follow Our Blessed Lady's Messages and follow her instructions."

Thank You so Much,

Susan

Lake City, FL

"Praying and fasting"

Prae

"No, we are not to judge, but we can be fruit inspectors! Thanks Friend of Medjugorje for doing just that. Heard on Truth Broadcasting—they have 10 radio stations in these states: NC, Utah, Iowa, Virginia. Contact them and ask them to read this letter over the air. I did. So many Catholics RINOS on all levels of government profane our faith to our embarrassment. We'll be doing another nine-day bread and water fast and three-hour Eucharistic Adoration. I had the grace of three hours of prayer today, but this is not always the case."

M.N.

Harrisonburg, VA

"Extraordinary!!! Brave and clear as it is will print it and go to my Bishop to give him a copy. If he does not speak English will offer him to translate in any form that would be needed. We must stop being cowards and letting our shepherds to be so!!! This false pandemic is taking so many out of discernment and Our Lady's messages are needed more than ever to convict and convert. Thanks a lot to a Friend of Medjugorje for this writing."

> *B.S.*
>
> *Cd. Obregon, Sonora, Mexico*

"Thank you, Friend of Medjugorje. It needed to be said. Unfortunately, they won't even bat an eye! Their only hope is for a sincere conversion at the time of the Warning which, by the way, is just around the corner. We all need to be strong now. Get to Confession... pray, pray, pray! Peace to all here."

> *Peter*
>
> *Montana*

"Everything I read is 1,000% true. God help our shepherds. They want to be popular among the people rather than say it like it is. Sin is sin no matter how you slice it."

> *M.S.*
>
> *Berlin, NJ*

"AMEN."

> *S.E.*
>
> *Traverse City, MI*

"Thank you for writing this. I agree with every word."

> *J.L.*
>
> *Knoxville, TN*

"Our Lady, definitely, spoke of politics at Fatima, she said consecrate Russia to her Immaculate Heart. First Fridays. First Saturdays. Our Lady obviously is political. And yes, Our Lady is a Trump supporter. If these people say otherwise it is because they are drinking fluoride

in the water. They might not be red pilled. Q is totally Christian. I believe the Mother of God is on the side of Trump. It's obvious if you have heard of the Weiner laptop that God, Himself, has stopped the evil one from the HRC third Obama administration. It's so plain that the Left is deceived."

Juliet

Chicago, IL

"Amen."

Angela

Columbus, OH

"Thank you! Excellent! I have never understood why such silence from our Church. May we listen to Her words and our Church open the doors to the Queen of Peace. Mother Mary be a Mother to me now."

A.

Miami, FL

"Thank you AFOM for your writings. I feel all are called with a special purpose, we are all soldiers of Christ and our Rosary is our sword."

Marianne

Rockport, IN

"Thank you for another great writing! I am going to send this out to several priests I know. We need Our Lady and Medjugorje more than ever!"

107

A.G.

Niagara Falls, NY

"As I have mentioned before: 'I'm worried about my judgement day
for transgressions that I was not aware are sins. How much more
the Bishops should be worried, they have received all the teachings
of Jesus!! Those of whom much is given, much is expected." I hope
that this writing is sent to ALL the bishops in the USA. They have
failed us miserably. May God have mercy on them. I will print this
out and send to my bishop and it will probably be read by a subordinate and then thrown away. I might believe them when they divest of
all their trappings, especially certain cardinals of which I am thinking. No more platitudes, DO SOMETHING CONCRETE. Stop
pillorying our beloved priests who do speak out!! Excommunicate
James Martin also, he is a wolf in sheep's clothing. Many more also!
I could say more, but I would just get 'worked up' all the more, and
AFOM says it much better than me. May Jesus have mercy on us!
Our Lady Queen of Peace, pray for us."

Kris

Ohio

"I just sent this text message to several friends: WOW! A Friend of
Medjugorje wrote and released a letter to the bishops this morning.
Someone in the comment section mentioned this podcast of February 2, 2019! I just finished listening. Remember St. Francis thought
he was to rebuild the physical Church and then he realized that it
was the internal Church that needed rescuing?! My thoughts after
reading AFOM's letter and listening to this podcast gives me the
sense that it is not a coincidence that we have a Francis in the Church

that is attempting to dismantle the teachings of the Catholic Church.
Our Lady is here to help us to renew the Church and She is using
AFOM, as a NEW Francis to counteract the destruction in order to
help Her reach Her apostles; Apostles Of the End Times to renew
the Church!!! What do you all think?"

M.S.

Paso Robles, CA

"Dear Friend of Medjugorje, you have given us an example of
standing up for your convictions, and yet respectfully, not judgingly.
May we all be able to stand up without fear. Lord, the next time I
am faced with danger for Your sake, let me remember that You are
faithful to reward Your people, no matter how much I may fear.
Amen! Isn't that the definition of courage! 'God's Word....is the...
Light of common sense.' (December 2, 2007) 'And the one on whom
seed was sown on good soil, this is the man who hears the word and
understands it; who indeed bears fruit and brings forth, some a hun-
dredfold, some sixty, and some thirty.' (Matthew 13:23) Medjugorje,
Caritas of Alabama is holy ground, I believe!! '...this time is my
time...' (January 25, 1997) Thank you Heavenly Father for the many
gifts of Graces through Your Son and His beautiful Mother."

J.O.

Lillington, NC

"Of the original 12 bishops—the 12 apostles—which one did not suf-
fer martyrdom? Of the original 12 bishops—the 12 apostles—which
one stood at the foot of the Cross with Our Sorrowful Mother—Our
Lady, knowing that at any minute he might be arrested and cruci-

109

fied with Our Lord? The answer to both questions is St. John. Ten apostles ran away in fear, one ran out and hanged himself. Stand with Our Lady at the foot of the Cross! AFTER Pentecost, the 12 bishops boldly proclaimed the Gospel, and later 11 suffered martyrdom. Bishops, do not wait until after the Warning to boldly proclaim Our Lady of Medjugorje."

J.K.

Las Vegas, NV

"Thank you, thank you, thank you! You have called a Spade a Spade and rightfully so! I will continue to pray for the bishops that they will be moved to action by the Holy Spirit as you have been all these years! Biden & Pelosi MUST be excommunicated! So many in the pews see this, yet the Bishops refuse to use the power given to them by Almighty God! I pray they heed this message! YOU, and a few holy priests, are what has kept me faithful to the Catholic faith all these years! I have longed for the Church of my youth, and a world where morality and truth within the Church were what convicted sinners. When we lost that, we lost the ability to see our own sins. Bishops included! God has given his Mother to us and She has given You to us! God Bless you, your family and the Community of Caritas!"

Julie

Fredericksburg, TX

"WILL THE BISHOPS EVEN HAVE THE BACKBONE TO READ THIS THROUGH??? Perhaps it could be read to them in the Confessional...Thank you AFOM for writing the words on many, many peoples' minds. May they ring from our lips to the shepherd's ears! May God have mercy on us all. Thank you, Caritas! All my love to Our Lady and to you!"

110

Lorraine

Micco, FL

"My heart has been so very heavy for so long as I have watched the downfall of the Church and I feel like a prisoner for my strong warrior feelings for Our Lady. I thank you so much for standing up to the Bishops for their retreatment to safeness!! I keep thinking about how did the people, who were in the crowds shouting Crucify Him on Friday and waving their palm branches the Sunday before, feel as the veils of hatred were lifted and they finally realized what they had done. We are right back there!! May God protect us to do what is needed to save souls."

G.P.

Gallatin, TN

"Amen.....that says it all."

Dianne

PA

"Amen! Perfectly explained. Spot on with the explanation of bishops and priests (our shepherds) regarding their tepidness toward Medjugorje and their political correctness; you have described the anger of all believers perfectly. I have always felt conflicted about having negative thoughts of someone holy, because we are taught it is a sin to say anything bad about a priest, pope or bishop. However, it is hard not to when they do not follow the Commandments themselves or make excuses (in my opinion) for those who would help them with power or image. I agree, Biden and Pelosi should be

excommunicated until they repent for their vile words and actions. Thank you!"

Maria

"God bless you and the Blessed Mother of Jesus. I look forward to your readings always. I wish I could make a trip to Medjugorje, but it will only be in my prayers. Please keep praying for all of us. Thank you!"

Susanne

Philadelphia, PA

"Thank you for your leadership in addressing our Shepherds. I wholeheartedly agree. Most of them have missed the time of their visitation. As a governing body, they have utterly failed us and firmly placed us in the cattle cars of the anti-human, antichrist globalist agenda, with which Biden is absolutely tied. The Red Dragon of communism has spread its errors over the whole world and is preparing to enslave us physically in addition to the spiritual enslavement of confused Catechesis (ie, "socialist justice") we have been enduring so long under the USCCB. Keep fighting. I unite my prayers and longings to yours."

L.T.

Dunlap, TN

"The Friend of Medjugorje is wise in this writing about the Church and the bishops. We are all sinner's and in need of repentance and forgiveness. I left the Roman Catholic Church right around the time the Blessed Virgin began appearing at Medjugorje for reasons I don't

care to divulge. Unfortunately, the bishops have bought into what the world has to offer rather than buying into the Word of God. I may be way off base when I say this, but I firmly believe that the reason none of the so called 'Catholics' who are in power in Washington D.C. is they are too powerful, and the bishops are afraid of losing their 501(c)(3) tax exempt status. All of us, no matter which religious denomination we belong to, need to focus on God and what an important role the Blessed Virgin Mary has played and continues to play in all of our lives. I pray that the bishop's come to their senses and believe that the apparitions of the Blessed Virgin are real and that they allow those sitting in the pews to come to know God's work in the world today. Blessings on your ministry."

T.M.

Palm Coast, FL

"Wow! I am so happy to have read this. Finally, a dumb slap in our faces to wake us up. It is all our faults that we are asleep in the pews. Because we let our bishops and priests not speak of, or to get us all involved in the hardest of subjects. We all need courage to defend our God-given human rights to life and liberty. Have no fear because our God is always near. Thank you to Mary our Loving Mother."

Vicki

MA

"WOW! This is AWESOME! Yes, I am copying and sending this to my local cardinal, former President Of the USCCB. Now is the time, backed by Our Lady through much, much prayer, penance, fasting and Her messages to show moral courage, No Matter What! Thank

113

you, Caritas and Terry Colafrancesco, for your faithful witness and convictions in this our great time of need! Thank you for your witness and tirelessly getting out those Great Messages. I am now clinging to them like a life preserver and through the Holy Rosary am now beginning to find peace amid sooo much confusion. This question has been on my mind lately, given all this horrible news of evil seeming to prevail everywhere, even in Holy Mother the Church. What does a Faithful Catholic do, where do I go, when even some of my seemingly faithful Catholic friends and my family, too seem to just lay down, lick their wounds, roll over and say, Well, it's 'God's Will.' Let's obey, put our mask on and go along to get along hoping and praying for better times. Our Lady's messages say different, as does this writing. Thanks for giving this poor soul a sense of direction and sooo much peace and joy! I am not afraid of whatever the future holds because in the end, 'Mary's Immaculate Heart Will Triumph' God's Love to Caritas, Our Lady's First Apostles"

L.S.

Houston, TX

"Amen. Also, I know of so many Catholics getting the coronavirus vaccine, that is tainted with aborted babies and has metals in it. (We have the Moderna one here.) Have had no direction or instruction from our bishop or priests. When I try to tell our friends, they don't believe me."

Renetta

KY

"AMEN and likewise for the bishops of Australia!"

M.T.

Elizabeth, Australia

"<u>Blind to your wrong</u> and deaf to the Holy Spirt it seems most shepherds seem to be . We all are on the via Dolorosa our Shepard Christ our Redeeming King went before us. As a lamb led to the slaughter. His example we are to follow. Three crosses on that hill our Savior with outstretched arms offered salvation to both. A free will choice to ask for forgiveness, one chooses wisely. Do we listen to the Truth revealed by the Holy Spirit? Do our bishops listen or are we being driven as sheep without shepherds into prediction by the devil and his minions? The Lion of Judah, Christ the Lamb of God will rule in His Glory. Our Queen and Mother is preparing His apostles for His return. May the Queen of Peace protect us with Her mantle. Thank you, Caritas, for stepping up and out in all that you do. Viva Cristo Rey!"

J.J.

Rock Hill, SC

"I sure hope all hear and listen and understand what you have been doing. I thank you from the bottom of my heart. I ask God for forgiveness. For strength to do His will. For courage to remain faithful. May the Queen of Peace reign soon, thank you Sweet Mary our Mother, thank you God our Father, thank you Jesus our Friend and Brother, and thank you Holy Spirit and May You dwell in us all. P.S. I love what you are doing! Blessing on you, thank you. Our Mother in Heaven and here on earth is so beautiful. I wish all to know Her, She loves and heals and helps everyone who ask. Thank you and thank Her and also the Father in Heaven for letting Her *come and stay with us She is the best Teacher in the whole wide world. Love and thanks."*

A.F.

Hemphill, TX

"Finally...thank you. Outstanding message."

Beth

Fishersville, VA

"Another awesome writing, direct from your heart to the world. It is time for me to grow some backbone and confront the bishops over here. I did a timid contact with the local priest not wanting to offend out of respect about one to two years ago that failed miserably. If this writing and a CD of one or two of the broadcasts doesn't wake them up, then I don't know what will. I will include my favorite that woke me up - the 2018 Special World Report 'Our Lady's Here Because Of What Is Coming Out Of The Church,' plus the one about Our Lady's Apostles mission mentioned in this writing called 'Fables, Bipolar, Church Leaders' from February 2019. Thank you AFOM, may God bless you and your family plus all at Caritas of Birmingham. I too believe the Secrets aren't too far away which will start to fix this big mess of a world. Thank you AFOM for listening to Our Lady's call and creating these broadcasts and writings. I look forward to them every week and will miss them when Our Lady's messages stop as assuming your mission may change then too."

David

Gillieston Heights, Australia

"I believe that no one genuinely wants to make mistakes. Unfortunately, they happen for a variety of reasons. And at this point, admit the mistakes, repent, and move quickly and do the right thing, before it is too late. Follow Mary and Her Messages. If one is in an important position, forget your reputation. What's more important your reputation or your eternal life? AFOM is extremely knowledgeable and has a deep understanding and insight into the messages. Maybe it's time to take him up on his offer to visit Caritas. Please, move quickly time is running out. God Bless to All."

Joanne

Livonia, MI

"I too am perplexed that the Catholic Church does not openly relay the messages of Our Lady. Does it not believe them to be true? It seems not. I too believe if these messages were spread throughout the Churches of the world, true conversion would happen on a mammoth scale and so many more people will be saved."

Michael Pater

Berwick, Victoria , Australia

"I support the recommendations and spiritual truths of this letter. These messages spoken by Our Blessed Mother are for everyone in our Church are critically important. As bishops, the shepherds of the Church, we need your leadership and guidance, listen to Mary or the consequences will be devastating."

Eduardo Fraga

Miami, FL

"Strength through courage, thank you Friend of Medjugorje."

Marvalee

Maricopa, AZ

"I agree wholeheartedly with you. We have been waiting...and waiting....and waiting for good priests, bishops, cardinals and the pope to stand for truth and we have not received it. Woe to them who could have spoken, but did not speak, who could have saved others, but did not take one action to save. Whitewashed tombs and filled with dead mans bones!"

Jeanette A. Coury

Houston, TX

"If all bishops stood together against the degradation and persecution of our Catholic faith that is happening not only in the secular world, but sadly also within our own Church, then many conversions would occur, and Catholics would once again have faith in their spiritual leaders."

Maria Eckl

Florence, AL

"THANK YOU, a Friend of Medjugorje, for this beautiful, necessary letter to our bishops. May they all read it prayerfully and take action. Our Lady has been waiting 40 years! May Jesus bless us all and help us to follow Blessed Mother with the Rosary in our hands. It's not too late. May God give us all the grace we need. God bless."

Mrs. Linda Marie Prince

Wilmington, DE

"Sign me up!"

Austin Blanchard

Sterrett, AL

"I Stand Strongly with a Friend of Medjugorje and all that is written here. TRUTH!!!"

Ruth McDonald

Sterrett, AL

"Thank you for saying what no one else in the world will say. I'm proud to be part of a Friend of Medjugorje's defining and leading the Medjugorje phenomenon for the entire world. Spread this. Start speaking up like a Friend of Medjugorje - tell your bishop and others that evil is evil and that stupid is stupid."

Jason Terrell

Caritas, Alabama

"Time for the bishops to act and time for those in the pew to demand it. If God can hear our cries and see that we repent, He will have mercy on us."

Alan Eckl

Florence , AL

"Bishops wake up before it's too late!"

Douglas Bourbina

Bloomington, IN—USA

"Thank you for all you do to promote Our Lady's message. I share all I learn with others. God be with you and Mary hold you in Her Immaculate Heart."

Jerinel Maynard

Dublin, OH

"Catholic Diocese of Jackson, MS, Bishop Joseph Kopacz, in reference to writing from a Friend of Medjugorje, January 19, 2021 A.D. 'Blind to Your Wrong' - Thank you for this!"

Maureen Murphy

Madison, MS

"This is a powerful and courageous message. Well worth the time to read it fully. Our bishops have truly failed us. May God bless those brave priests who have visited Medjugorje and spread Our Lady's messages."

June Downey

Grant Park, IL

"I agree, bishops need to stand up against abortion, same sex unions, gender confusion, Socialism, Communism, etc. They need to listen to our Mother. Medjugorje is real and Our Lady's messages are true and for our salvation."

Donald Wires

Loveland, OH

"Praying this message is heard and understood."

Bridgette Barnhart
Saint Louis, MO

"Better late than never."

Frances Bigeni
Central Coast, NSW, Australia

"You said it perfectly! Thank you for being the voice of the peasants in the pews: Our Lady Apostles of Love."

Jihane Allen
Okotoks, Alberta, Canada

"Amen. Excellent writing and so true."

Robert McLeer
Lawrenceville, GA

"Thank you for your spiritual nourishment with Our Lady's message given through the visionaries of Medjugorje."

Art Zavala
Anaheim, CA

"May Our Lord hear the cry of His people and covert our shepherds back to the day they fell in love to serve Christ and His people."

Patty Morales
Humble, TX

"Bishops, we need you. Please stand up for injustice. Be led by Our Blessed Mother."

Georgene Brook

Redmond, OR

"Praying for the bishops to see the injustice they are doing to all the people they are to be leading to their Eternal Home. I have often felt if it is alright for these, so called, Catholic leaders when they do not speak out against the blasphemy of Biden, Pelosi and others receiving the most Holy Sacrament. It should be justified then that anyone of other faiths can receive the Eucharist as well."

Barbara Wilson

Boerne, TX

"I am tired of listening to sermons that have no meat every week but when are we going to hear what we need to hear regarding how to live our faith in this dark time. Why are we praying for the vaccine during the prayers after the Creed? Why is it ok for people to be maskless at the Latin Mass and receive on the tongue but not ok during the Ordus Novo Mass? Why has the Church never outwardly thanked President Trump but in my Church's bulletin asking to pray for President Elect Biden? Really? I decided after USBBC congratulated Biden as president elect, I wrote my bishop and told him take me off the mailing list for Annual Bishop's Appeal...I am done giving to the Church that is not serving the needs of the people. I had a conversion experience with Our Lady of Medjugorje and credit Her for leading me to Her Son Jesus. I was a cradle born Catholic, but I've learned more from a Friend of Medjugorje than my own parish priest. I am proud to say I am an apostle of Our Lady and will be a Child of Light."

Francine Amy

Vera Beach, FL

"Our Lady, Queen of Peace, pray for us! God bless all of you at Caritas of Birmingham for your brave and faithful witness to our Blessed Mother and Her peace plan from Heaven. May this beautiful plea be heard and listened to by our bishops!"

Regina McMahon

Cochranville, PA

"Yes, please add my name. And yes, I will need strength and courage. Thank you for doing this for us in the pews."

Elvira Lowe

Woodbridge, VA

"Very powerful and true."

Cathy Tharp

Bardstown, KY

"WOW! I feel so blessed to have gone to Medjugorje with Caritas and been a part of something so profound! I will always remember how a Friend of Medjugorje stressed to the pilgrims to use every minute wisely. While reading this writing, my heart was on fire with conviction. I wanted to shout out to the whole world how real Medjugorje is (Mary's Israel)!! Your words are so convicting and so full of Truth! Thank you for being so courageous to stand up and speak the TRUTH! WE, the peasants in the pew, needed to hear these words! Praying for our bishops to awaken and be courageous!

Thank you again, a Friend of Medjugorje, for an OUTSTANDING 'A+++' writing! AMEN!"

Connie Thomas

Harwood, TX

"I stand with Terry!!! May I have the might to spread this message!!"

Dan Kremer

Yorkshire, OH

"I pray for Archbishop Thomas Rodi and for my parish priest, Fr. David Shoemaker. I ask for the intercession of my childhood priest, Fr. Killian Mooney, who took a group of us to Caritas in the '80s."

Mary Boyce

Eufaula, AL

"Please, bishops, be true followers of the Lord, and true sons of Mary – the Warrior Queen and Gentle Mother. She has a plan to lead you and all people back to Her Son."

Lisa Evans

Marysville, WA

"I agree with everything that you wrote. I feel blessed that you are standing up for what is the truth."

Earline Kraemer

Vacherie, LA

"You spoke the truth. Our bishops must stand for truth as Jesus did when He was here. Pray for our bishops to have courage and not to be afraid of what people will say or do and follow Mary's words."

124

"Excellent writing."

"I totally agree with this writing by a Friend of Medjugorje, especially the part about standing up against the policies promoting abortion and

"I totally agree with this writing by a Friend of Medjugorje, especially the part about standing up against the policies promoting abortion and abominable marriage and socialism and condemning the policies of Joe Biden and others. We need our leaders to lead!"

"May God, through the intercession of Our Lady Queen of Peace, have mercy on us."

"For the state of my soul and those around me, I feel I need to see and discern all that Mother Mary has said over the last 40 years at Medjugorje. This is a grace that should not be ignored and I don't intend to."

"Unfortunately, our shepherds are silent. Thank you for giving us voice. I agree with you. Thank you."

Eugene Morales

Humble, TX

"Thank you for all that you do for the continued motivation to stay on our Salvation Course!"

Laura Miller

Breaux Bridge, LA

"I wish our Churches were overflowing and people would come together in great numbers to pray. Rip off the masks, fill the pews, and keep the faith!!! We had one priest tell us to not come to Church if we are not wearing a mask. I love Church. I no longer feel comfortable there. I keep going."

Rachelle Blackman

Deland, FL

"I am a Permanent Deacon in Brigantine, New Jersey, and I am all in!"

Leonard Long

Galloway, NJ

"Promise to fast more, pray more and stay true to my Lord by following the Ten Commandments. I pray for all our priests and all my brothers and sisters in Christ and especially those who do not believe and are causing havoc, those who are lukewarm in their faith

and those who are not practicing Catholics. Thank you, our Dear Blessed Mother and Holy Trinity."

Marie Ram
Chino Hills, CA

"Bishops, wake up and lead us."

Marge Barton
Fenton, MO

"Thank you for this writing!"

Jodie Faltysek
East Bernard, TX

"Thank you, a Friend of Medjugorje, for this much needed writing. I pray our bishops will read it all and act on it. I am so disgusted and disheartened by most of the leaders in the Church. I trust in our Lord Jesus Christ and I believe in the messages of our Blessed Mother. O Mary, conceived without sin, pray for us who have recourse to thee. Crush the plans of satan under your heel. God bless all of you at Caritas."

Jeri Gumerson
Greenwood, IN

"The information stated in the letter to the US bishops needed to be said to them. Only hope they will pay attention, open their souls to the Queen of Peace and change."

Daniel Kortes
New Baltimore, MI

"I cannot believe any bishop would give Communion to anyone who approves abortion."

Jackie Ramnarong
Fort Wayne, IN

"Time and thought was given to this writing…a well written writing. As I was reading this, I was thinking of all the years of praying the 7-7-7 prayers for our bishops. They truly are blind in many ways. Blind in that they cannot see how we truly need them to lead us. Blind in how we have waited for them to take a lead for so long. Blind in their call. Blind in that their flocks wait to no avail, hoping beyond hope. AVAIL…do you realize the Latin meaning of that world…from Latin valere be strong, be of value. I guess that says it all. Thank you, a Fiend of Medjugorje for penning this. The Holy Spirit inspired you perfectly in showing their blindness."

Sherry Hittle
Ida Grove, IA

"Our leaders have been too silent in confronting our Washington politicians and their using their Catholic Faith to make themselves seem righteous; then openly putting forth their plans to openly promote murder; injustice and evil! JMJ, save us from ourselves."

Teresa Thompson
Rock Hill, SC

"God bless you!"

Peggy Wojcik
Columbus, NE

128

"A powerful writing and message for all bishops and all clergy. You cannot be on the fence. You must pick the light or the darkness. By your silence you are making a decision for the darkness and taking others with you."

> Susan
>
> Conway, CA

"Queen of Peace Please bless all."

> Dee Logsdon
>
> Springfield, KY

"I learned so much from your message. I applaud you for your words. I wish our priests would speak out against what is going on today: the late-term abortions in New York, the laws passed In California."

> Janice Hirsch
>
> Odell, IL

"Please bishops, sand up for the teachings of Our Lord Jesus Christ. I am no one, but I am everyone who is watching their beloved Catholic Church fall into ruin. We need you to shepherd us, His flock. We will stand with you in His Truth. You are under the protection of Our Lady's Mantle. Be not afraid."

> Deb
>
> Romeoville, IL

"Wow, if this writing doesn't convict the bishops and priests of how their silence is misleading their flocks, I don't know what will.

Specially not calling out Biden, Pelosi, and the rest as poor Catholic examples for the country and the world. God bless you for always speaking the truth and not being afraid. My prayer group is always praying for our priests and bishops and the pope to know the Truth. I pray this works."

> *Mary Rausser*
> *Somers, NY*

"Thank you, Mary, Mother of God. God's Will be done on earth as it is in Heaven."

> *Lois Opincar*
> *Avon Lake, OH*

"I support the request to accept Medjugorje as true and authentic. I ask the USCCB to join in this acceptance NOW!"

> *Kathy Winner*
> *Minster, OH*

"WOW! Thank you for making everything crystal clear! You have not judged, but rather courageously rebuked our Church leaders. I pray that they will ask for the intercession of St. Romero, who abandoned his comfortable priesthood and became the voice of the people.

"If Jesus, the Son of God, was obedient to Mary and Joseph, who are we not to do the same, especially those who were given authority within the Church! So, I dare to say – not if, but when our Church leaders choose to run to Our Lady, Queen of Peace, She will multiply the graces, undo the knots, and usher in an era of peace! God bless us all!"

Carolyn Montenegro

Hopewell Junction, NY

"Thank you and God bless you!"

Mychelle Davis

Elllijay, GA

"This writing powerfully defines what many of us have been feeling."

Jill Finkenbine

Maplewood, OH

"Thank you, a Friend of Medjugorje, for the good work you are doing for Mother Mary the Queen of Peace. We keep on praying that Her plans may be realized. Thank you for guidance and we shall continue to pry for our shepherds who are lost."

Kamanzi May Faustina

Kampala, Uganda, Africa

"Our Lady Queen of Peace bless Caritas for their courage and deep faith in God's promises. God have mercy on your people and humble us that we may be exulted for the greater glory of God the Father, God the Son and God the Holy Spirit. Thank you, Mama Mary, for leading us! Amen!"

Monica Vigil

Espanola, NM

"God bless America! One nation UNDER GOD, indivisible with liberty and justice for ALL! We must all unite in prayer. Jesus, I trust in You!"

131

Peggy Gleason
Shakopee, MN

"Pray for us who fail you."

Cynthia Gabaldon
La Verne, CA

"I am praying, have been praying the Rosary every day since my mother died March 30, 2020. I did the nine-day bread and water fast…I am praying all the time for our Mother Mary to help us. My mother and grandmother were very devoted to Her…Thank you for all you do and all your information. God Bless You All."

Barbara Heizmann
Oak Hill, FL

"Amen!"

Ann Willenbring
Richmond, MN

"For years I had questions about what some bishops were saying or not doing. This is evidence that my and others' fears were not unfounded. I'll be praying and fasting that the bishops that need them will be humble and courageous enough to repent and have God smiling on them once again. Stay strong, Friend of Medjugorje, and Thank you."

Margaret Grossman
Benson, MN

"Add my name to the list for the bishops."

Susana G. Fullerton

Kents Store, VA

"Thank you, Friend of Medjugorje! My love and prayers are with you and the Community."

Sharon Allende

Fountain Valley, CA

"Absolutely wonderful article and filled with truth. I am ashamed in front of non-Catholics to call our current politicians 'Catholic.' How outrageous! Shepherds need to lead their flock with powerful sermons and not get quiet at election time (orders from the bishops) because of fear of being 'political.' Life is the most important issue, period."

Barbara Heagy

Milton, DE

"To the bishops, understand the time has come! You were chosen to shepherd His people, but you have become another Judas of our times. Mary called out to Judas in his day, but he would not listen, your actions of nonaction condemns you. You have not recognized the time of your visitation. Otherwise, you would have repented and turned from your wicked ways. St. Michael the Archangel said to lucifer, God be your Judge. So I, as a Friend of Medjugorje, say the same to you!"

Kathie Jackson

Tulsa, OK

"I am totally in agreement with the recent letter by a Friend of Medjugorje to the bishops in the USCCB. Thank you, Friend of

Medjugorje, for expressing the courage of your convictions and for all you have done to spread Our Lady's messages. May we all go forward as Mary's apostles and carry on with the work She has entrusted to us, and continue to pray for our families, our communities and our nations, as She has requested."

Donna Cummings
Mechanicsville, IA

"Truly a wake-up call for our bishops and priests! Finally, the truth!... We wouldn't be experiencing the chaos in our country if we had followed Our Mother's messages in Medjugorje...May God have mercy on us!"

Janice Tidmarsh
Cave Creek, AZ

"How can I get information to talk to pastors about allowing Medjugorje information in Church?"

Geralyn Suhor
New Orleans, LA

"I agree with everything a Friend of Medjugorje said. Those government officials who are Catholic and support abortion and abominable relationships should be excommunicated and denied the Eucharist."

Pam Coulon
Gonzales, LA

"Come Holy Spirit Come! We have been stopped even in a neutral space, from publicly distributing Our Lady's Messages, gifts from our family, not from our parish. Our priest allowed us to have private conversations with others, but stopped any public distribution. Our bishop read and enjoyed reading <u>They Fired the First Shot 2012</u>. He mentioned that it contained Truth and was still on his bookshelf. But, the next time he visited, he wouldn't accept any Medjugorje information, despite having visited Medjugorje personally while traveling in Europe and having recognized Truth coming from Medjugorje. We have had parishioners explain how we were not in line with Church teaching, only to have a random website with someone's opinion condemning the entire movement as their evidence. Forty years is long enough. The fruits of Medjugorje stand for themselves. I don't need to hear a priest give a homily on Medjugorje, I would just appreciate support to be able to tell people why/how Our Lady has impacted my life. To be able to share messages that have convicted me. To be able to share this Fire that was set ablaze after hearing Her words. A Fire of immeasurable compassion, empathy, and love for souls.. There are so many who are afraid to even hear about Our Lady's words, because they are under the impression that they could somehow be tricked or deceived. Pope Francis has allowed official pilgrimages to Medjugorje. Dynamic Catholic is starting their first pilgrimage to Medjugorje. There are years worth of scientific proof available. What else do you need? Why not listen to Her words yourselves? Why not see what others are talking about? Why only read the reviews about Her without experiencing/judging Her yourself? So many people have, in love, tried to talk our family out of following Our Lady. They point out all of the good our

family does for others, but how we have been led down a bad path. I patiently remind them that our family is who we are because of Our Lady. We have gone through and daily continue to go through conversion. We are called to be a reflection of Christ. We are a reflection of what we have learned from Our Lady, making us a better reflection of Her Son. Going to Confession is hard. Taking cold showers is hard. Ripping band-aids off is hard. But like the band-aid, there are things that are better to do without weighing out the consequences. Be Bold Bishops! Take a stand for your diocese; defend your flock; be clear about supporting Our Lady of Medjugorje! Our Lady said that there is still time. Seize the moment!

Michael Capelle
Caledonia, MS

"I stand with Our Lady The Queen of Peace and the Friend of Medjugorje, our Blessed Mother has always been the catalyst and conduit for God's plan. She, in great humility, said YES to bring our salvation the WORD her Son Our Lord Jesus Christ. She suffered His Death and Passion in full knowledge of Who Jesus is. Our Lord, out of great love sends His Mother again, and we ignore Her. Blessed Mother Mary spends Her time in Heaven in TEARS interceding on behalf of poor sinners, and we thank Her by rejecting Her Son, Her Spouse the Holy Spirit and the Will of God our Father. She spends Her Heaven in tears. I will pray more urgently, work harder to repent of my sins, I promise to incorporate nine days of fasting and other penance in great HOPE that our Shepherds do not delay further. May the Holy Spirit guide us and bless us to fulfill HIS will."

Maureen Ann Redler
Decatur, AL

136

"Please read carefully and pray about this letter. Your Church is dying. We need your leadership!"

Margaret Solimene

East Hartford, CT

"Que viva Cristo Rey!"

Cynthia

Edinburg, Texas

"Thank you! Mama Mary Queen of Peace! May God's Will be done!"

Jacqueline Robinson

Barrie, Ontario, Canada

"Thank you for speaking the truth. We need courageous bishops to lead!! God bless America. God bless the World. Jesus I Trust in You"

Karen Fagan

Dover, MA

"I agree with 'Blind to Your Wrong.'"

Steve Craig

Orange Grove, TX

Endnotes

1. The Victory Channel, "Run to the Roar," David Barton, January 10, 2021.
2. https://www.ncronline.org/news/opinion/distinctly-catholic/gomezs-lack-leadership-full-display-statement-biden.
3. One Voice, Birmingham Diocese of Alabama, December 11, 2020, pg. 5.
4. https://www.churchmilitant.com/news/article/st.-louis-de-montfort-the-last-days.
5. Ibid.
6. Ibid.
7. Ibid.
8. Ibid.
9. https://usccb.org/issues-and-action/faithful-citizenship/upload/forming-consciences-for-faithful-citizenship-2007.pdf, p. 11.
10. A Friend of Medjugorje, What Does Our Lady Have to Do with It? Everything,", December 2020.
11. https://www.americamagazine.org/politics-society/2020/09/17/catholic-biden-trump-faithful-citizenship-election.
12. https://twitter.com/Sachinettiyil/status/1343965794149888000.
13. Ibid.

THE BOOK, YOU WON'T HEAR ABOUT FROM THE PULPIT, THAT HAS CHANGED AND SAVED TENS OF THOUSANDS OF MARRIAGES AROUND THE WORLD.

How to Change Your Husband

Owner's Manual for the Family
By a Friend of Medjugorje

THE COMPLETE BISHOP'S SET

$~~36~~$ ^{95} 62% SET DISCOUNT

13^{95}

Included in this Set:

A complete set of short books, the book and audio CDs by a Friend of Medjugorje to help yourself or others understand the direction the bishops have allowed our Church and nation to go. The blocking of the Medjugorje apparitions, and what is possible when clergy collaborate in the spirit of prayer with elected officials.

1. <u>Blind to Your Wrong</u>
2. "Quietism"
3. "Will You Miss Out on the Second Greatest Moment in Time"
4. "So You're Waiting for Church Approval?"
5. "You Cannot Spread Medjugorje?"
6. "We Must Go to A Higher Truth"
7. "Bishop's Imprudent Prudence"
8. "The Sin of Waiting"
9. "Never in History"
10. "What Does Our Lady Have to Do With It? EVERYTHING"
11. "…You See for Yourselves, that with our prayers, all Evils are Destroyed…"
12. "Crimes: Silence, Bad Teachings and Something Diabolical"
13. "A Forecast of satan's Plans" Audio CD
14. "Take Us to Jail" Audio CD
15. "Time to Unmake" Audio CD

The **Corona Vision**
Will Instantly Change Your Life

A book by a Friend of Medjugorje that is sweeping the nation.

$4.00 each book. As low as $1.00 each book for cases of 100.

See the order form in the back of the book to order.

"…The words you speak are riveting. I see, my son sees…"

—Suzanne—Freehold, New Jerse

CHANGE THE CHURCH WITH A SHIRT

peasants in
the pews

$6 each

See Order Form in Back to Order
or go to mej.com and click on "Shop Online"

145

146

Order Form

		Shipping and Handling Options	
Blind to Your Wrong Soft Cover Books BF129	*Please add shipping and handling* ☐ **1**=$6.95 ☐ **10**=$40.00 ($4.00 EA) (For case pricing see below.)		$
How to Change Your Husband Soft Cover BF103	*Please add shipping and handling* ☐ **1**=$6.00 ☐ **10**=$40.00 ($4.00 EA) (For larger quantities call for discounted case pricing.)		$
The Complete Bishop's Set SET1010	*Please add shipping and handling* ☐ **1**=$13.95 ☐ **5**=$69.75 ($13.95 EA) ☐ **2**=$27.90 ($13.95 EA) ☐ **OTHER**=___ ($13.95 EA)		$
The Corona Vision Soft Cover Books BF126	*Please add shipping and handling* ☐ **1**=$4.00 ☐ **10**=$30 ($3.00 EA) ☐ **25**=$50 ($2.00 EA) ☐ **50**=$75 ($1.50 EA) (For larger quantities call for discounted case pricing.)		$
"Patriotic Rosary" Short Books BK1005	*Suggested Donation (Please add shipping and handling)* ☐ **1**=FREE please add s&h ☐ **50**=$30.00 (60¢ EA) ☐ **10**=$9.00 (90¢ EA) ☐ **100**=$40.00 (40¢ EA) ☐ **25**=$18.75 (75¢ EA) ☐ **1,000**=$300.00 (30¢ EA)		$
The David Answer Soft Cover Books BF128	*Please add shipping and handling* ☐ **1**=$7.00 ☐ **10**=$40.00 ($4.00 EA) (For larger quantities call for discounted case pricing.)		$

Item #	Size	Color (Black or Natural)	Qty.	$6.00 each (add $2 each for XXL)	
TS105				**Peasants in the Pews T-Shirt**	$

				Subtotal	$

Shipping & Handling

Order Sub-total	UPS SurePost *(Standard)*	UPS Ground
$0-$10.00	$8.00	$15.00
$10.01-$20.00	$10.50	$17.50
$20.01-$50.00	$13.00	$20.00
$50.01-$100.00	$20.00	$27.00
Over $100.00	20% of total	25% of total

For overnight delivery, call for pricing.
***International (Surface):
Double above shipping Cost.
Call for faster International delivery. $

Blind to Your Wrong CASES OF 36 BOOKS
For Affordable, Easy Convenience

BF129–CASE CASES OF 36 ($1.75 EA)

$63 + $45 S&H = $108.00

(UPS Shipping is included)

	Cases	QTY.	TOTAL	
☐	1	36	$108.00	
☐	2	72	$216.00	
☐ OTHER	_____		($108.00 EA)	$

	TOTAL:	$

☎ Ph: (Outside USA add 001)
205-672-2000 ext. 315 USA 24 hrs.
🖷 Fax: **205-672-9667 USA 24 hrs.**
✉ Mail: **Caritas of Birmingham**
100 Our Lady Queen of Peace Drive
Sterrett, AL 35147-9987 USA

Enclose in remittance envelope or call in your order and donation.
If you have any questions you may call 205-672-2000 and leave a message on ext. 315.
Or call during office hours 8:30 a.m.–5:00 p.m. Central Time
Monday–Friday and talk with a real person ☺
The Federal Tax Exempt I.D. # for Caritas of Birmingham is 63-0945243.

Ship to: Name(s) *(please print)* _____ Birthday: _____

Address _____

City _____ State _____ Zip Code _____

Phone # _____(if an international number, include all digits)

☐ Payment Enclosed

Credit Card type (check one) ☐ *VISA*   ☐ *MasterCard*   ☐ *Discover*

Credit Card Number _____   3-Digit Code on Back: _____

Expiration date: _____ - _____   e-mail: _____

Cut or Copy ✂ or Send Same information

Job 2989 2/15/2021